THE
ALBERT
MEMORIAL

The Anarchist Life and Times of Albert Meltzer
(7 January 1920–7 May 1996)

THE ALBERT MEMORIAL

The Anarchist Life and Times of Albert Meltzer
(7 January 1920–7 May 1996)

An Appreciation by Phil Ruff
Second edition

With an introduction by John Patten and postscripts by Albert Meltzer, 'Acrata', Stuart Christie and other comrades

First published 1997 by The Meltzer Press, Hastings
Published as an ebook 2014 by ChristieBooks, Hastings:
http://www.christiebooks.com/ChristieBooksWP/

2nd edition published 2016 by AK Press and the Kate
Sharpley Library
ISBN: 978-1-84935-280-2

Kate Sharpley Library
BM Hurricane
London WC1N 3XX
UK
www.katesharpleylibrary.net

AK Press
370 Ryan Ave. #100 Chico, CA 95973
www.akpress.org
akpress@akpress.org

AK Press
33 Tower St. Edinburgh EH6 7BN Scotland
www.akuk.com
ak@akedin.demon.co.uk

Additional note about photos: Thanks to Phil Ruff, Stuart
Christie, and Col Longmore for providing photos. Please
contact them via the Kate Sharpley Library to arrange
permission for commercial use. Cover image credits:
Front, Albert Meltzer by Ken Sutherland. Back: Red and
black flags at Albert Metzer's funeral by Col Longmore.

CONTENTS

Obituaries of Albert Meltzer described him as a 'torch-bearer of international Anarchism.' What makes an Anarchist torchbearer? His international links across his years of activism are clear in his autobiography 'I Couldn't Paint Golden Angels': he worked with comrades from India, China, Sweden, Spain, Australia, the USA... But beyond that he fought, in theory and practice, for Anarchism to be a living movement.

Politics: It doesn't always do what it says on the tin!

Albert was often accused of 'sectarianism' because he opposed the idea of an 'open door policy' for Anarchism: that anyone claiming to be an Anarchist should be taken at their word. He was never prepared to let bad definitions drive out good without an argument.

He defended the Anarchist heritage of resistance against the reworked liberalism which idealised 'perpetual protest.' In the relatively free sixties, some argued that revolutionary change was old hat, and that we should be content with 'living as freely as possible' in the here and now. Albert was very sarcastic about how emphasising Anarchism as an abstract idea allowed authoritarian scum like Thatcher to pose as libertarians.

He also opposed what he called the 'package-deal Left', sadly still in evidence today, where having a 'line' which can be used to march the papersellers to the top of the hill, and the next and the next, takes the place of principles or the idea of human liberation.

A Class Act

As a trade union activist and working class militant, Albert was a firm believer in class struggle Anarchism, not as a ghetto within a ghetto, but as the best bet for defending our current freedom and achieving long-term change. His faith in the potential of the working class was unshaken by the shocking revelation that some of them were not angels: his twofold response was that, having no need to exploit another class, they had the greatest libertarian potential and (more humorously) that the only place angels would have to be involved in workers control was in heaven!

One of his aims in the many books and hundreds of articles he wrote was to encourage a 'Monday militancy' – to struggle for freedom in every area of our lives, rather than just chanting about it on the weekend.

A quote from 'The Floodgates of Anarchy' (co-written with Stuart Christie) shows that he was open-minded about the need for flexibility of tactics:

> We must accept reforms in the spirit in which they are offered, and, if, in order to get a political

prisoner released after twenty years in jail, we were asked to appear in our shirts like the burghers of Calais, and march around a cathedral carrying a penitential candle, this would be an act of solidarity no less than attacking a Spanish bank or kidnapping an ambassador. [...]

What would be the grossest superstition – and this is the analogy with reformism – is to believe that simply by appearing in sackcloth and ashes and traipsing around the cathedral, the dictator could be persuaded to release the prisoners. [...] Letters to members of parliament, discussions of civil rights and the abstract rights of man, petitions to the United Nations, public statements for which one must angle for 'names', the collecting of thousands of ordinary signatures ... all these are secular, democratic versions of the sackcloth and ashes, required by the despot. We may need to engage in them, we may benefit from them, but we do not have to be fooled by them.

The Anarchist Black Cross: Anarchy in Action

Spanish Anarchists were the staunchest opponents of Franco's fascist regime, yet in or out of jail received the least international support. This changed with the imprisonment of Stuart Christie, jailed in 1964 for his part in a plot to assassinate Franco. The spotlight illuminated not only him, but the fact of Anarchist resistance and the fate of other Anarchist prisoners. Albert helped behind the scenes efforts to 'encourage' Stuart's release. Once freed in 1967 he joined with Albert to launch the Anarchist Black Cross, to call for solidarity with those left behind. This solidarity gave practical help (food and medicine) to the prisoners, and helped force the Spanish state to apply its own parole rules. Just as importantly, it introduced activists elsewhere to a revolutionary tradition very different from the murderous and authoritarian Russian one. One of the first prisoners the Anarchist Black Cross helped free was Miguel García, a veteran of the Spanish Anarchist resistance, as well as wartime resistance in France. After serving 20 years (to the hour!) in Spanish jails he moved to London to work with the ABC – and inspiring a new generation of activists.

The Anarchist Black Cross was always beset by people with bright plans for expansion ('why not aid all victims of capitalism everywhere?') regardless of the resources needed. Giving the chance for people to provide direct solidarity, it achieved more than many paper organisations and still shows the value of practical Anarchist activism.

Keep the Black Flag flying here...

Speaking of paper, the ABC bulletin became *Black Flag*, at times weekly, and at others 'excitingly irregular', which has for 30 years pushed the idea and practice of revolutionary Anarchism. In the early 1980s it reinvigorated yet another generation of Anarchist politics in Britain. By connecting with young working class Anarchists coming from the punk scene it helped spread new energy and attitude. These were the people who went on to spread Anarchist ideas more widely than they had been seen for years in the miners' and other strikes, as well as the fight against the Poll Tax.

Legacy

Anarchists of today, if they ever wonder what one person can do, could learn a lot from the life of Albert Meltzer. Albert has left many legacies to the Anarchist movement, from a frank and justified scepticism of the value of academic 'experts' on or media exposes about Anarchism, to a supply of scathing anecdotes about most political ideologies.

Many of the projects he was involved with carry on: *Black Flag* is still promoting Anarchist resistance and the Kate Sharpley Library continues uncovering the grassroots history of the movement, which is, after all, where its strength has always lain. A publishing house (The Meltzer Press) set up in tribute to him has produced some important historical works including the first English translation of Peirats' classic account of 'The CNT in the Spanish Revolution'.

A political appreciation like this inevitably leaves out much that could be said – especially of a life so full. To many people Albert truly was an Anarchist torch-bearer (and not only to radicals: Special Branch called him 'the doyen of the British Anarchist movement'!). To many others who worked or communicated with him, he carried other sparklers of humour and com-radeship. He had no time for the cult of 'great men' or 'great women' in isolation from the movements that made them what they were, so perhaps the best tribute is to say that he was part of a long line of comrades who devoted their lives to spreading the idea of Anarchism and proving the worth of its principles in the fight for human freedom.

John Patten
July 2002

This article was first published in *Freedom* to mark the 'end of hostilities' between Freedom Press and class struggle anarchists around *Black Flag*, which were possibly at their worst immediately following Albert's death. *Freedom* v.63, n.16 (10 August 2002). Freedom Press can be found at 84b Whitechapel High St, London, E1 7QX and https://freedompress.org.uk/ (July 2016).

ALBERT MELTZER
by Phil Ruff

ALBERT MELTZER was born in 1920, into a mixed Jewish-Irish Protestant family in Tottenham, a northern district of London.

He discovered his own brand of stateless socialism while still at school, but came into the anarchist movement, at the age of 15, through amateur boxing. A protégé of the socialist boxers Andy Newton and Johnny Hicks at their famous gymnasium in Edgware Road, near Paddington, Albert met his match in the ring with a young anarchist seaman from Glasgow, Wilson 'Billy' Campbell. Billy had learnt both boxing and anarchism from Frank Leech, a well-known Glasgow anarchist, and also had contacts in the seafarers' union of the Spanish National Confederation of Labour, the CNT, in Bilbao. He and Albert became best friends and through Billy Albert joined the main anarchist organisation in London at the time, the Freedom Group, whose most prominent member was George Cores.

Many years later, Albert was to write of Billy, who was drowned when his ship was torpedoed in 1940, 'Wilson Campbell ... was every way an anarchist. I don't just say this because he was a dear friend, but now when people ask which anarchist influenced me most, Bakunin or Kropotkin or whoever, I just don't talk their language when I say Billy Campbell.'[1]

True to his influence, at the first anarchist meeting he attended, at the National Trade Union Club in New Oxford Street, London, in 1935, Albert spoke up in defence of boxing, which was being denounced by the Russian revolutionist Emma Goldman.

When in 1936 the Spanish workers rose against Franco's coup, Albert was still at school, though since the leaving age was lower then, many of his contemporaries would have left. He plunged at once into solidarity work, helping Emma Goldman and Leah Feldman* (*see below*) to collect money and garments for the Spanish anti-fascists.[2]

Also at this time, Albert joined a group that was contriving to send illegal shipments of arms to the Spanish anarchists. The prime mover in this activity was Captain Jack White; three shiploads of arms reached Bilbao before the operation was blown. The export company set up by White was based at an impressive sounding address in Soho Square, but was actually the attic workroom of the anarchist tailor Alf Rosenbaum. Albert was characteristically downbeat about his role in the operation: 'my part was peripheral, consisting of invoice typing and listening to White endlessly relating the crimes of the Catholic church.'[3] Nevertheless, it was a formative experience for the young anarchist, and Albert's quiet commitment to deliver practical aid to the Spanish anarchists remained constant for the rest of his life.

> ## * Leah Feldman (1899–1993)
>
> BORN in Warsaw, Leah left Poland as a girl to break from her orthodox Jewish parents and to be active in the London Yiddish-speaking anarchist workers' movement. She made her own way to Moscow after the 1917 revolution, attended Kropotkin's funeral in 1921 and joined Nestor Makhno's anarchist Insurgent Army in Ukraine, fighting Whites and Reds alike. Escaping to Germany Leah worked with the Anarchist Black Cross in Berlin on behalf of prisoners in Russia, before returning to London where Albert met her in 1935. Despite a sentimental attachment to *Freedom* (which she never read), Leah remained committed to the practice of revolutionary activism, safehousing arms and explosives for the First of May Group in the 1960s, taking part in the international campaign to save Irish anarchists Noel and Marie Murray from hanging in 1975/76, and attending the 1984 Congress of the AIT/IWA in Madrid. Albert scattered Leah's ashes at the Chicago Martyrs' Memorial. He describes her in his memoirs as a 'constant leitmotif in my experiences of the movement'.

From the start of his revolutionary involvement, Albert always believed that the anarchist movement suffered from a lack of organisation and a lack of action. In January 1937 with Billy Campbell and others, he formed an affinity group, i.e. a body of like-minded comrades to carry out specific tasks.

Calling themselves 'The Friends of Durruti' after the then recently deceased Spanish militant (they were the *first* group, Albert claimed, to use that name), they undertook early in their existence the burning down of a stand glorifying Franco at a British fascist exhibition (for which Albert earned the distinction of being denounced by Emma Goldman as 'a young rascal and hooligan').

After the Barcelona May Days of the same year, when the Catalan anarchist organisation of the same name emerged to fight the communist coup and terror, Albert's group changed its name to 'Revolutionary Youth' and began publishing a bulletin called *The Struggle*, later joining another group in South-West London to form the 'Libertarian Youth Movement'.

Albert was also active in the pre-war anti-Nazi underground in Germany, and was involved with one attempt (organised by the 'Schwarzrot'[4] anarchist group in Birmingham) to assassinate Hitler in 1938. Even with a British passport, travelling to Nazi Germany with false papers for Hitler's assassin was not the safest of pastimes for a half-Jewish anarchist, but Albert was never short of daring. He actually risked his life and liberty rather a lot over the years, and his autobiography (written with an eye to avoiding prosecution) frequently plays down his real contribution to anarchist resistance activities. On this occasion, Albert safely made contact with Willy Fritzenkotter and Hilda Monte, two of the most outstanding 'unsung heroes' of the German Resistance, who as well as organising a number of attempts on Hitler's life, were behind an attempt to shoot Goering. (A female member of the action group had somehow acquired an official invitation to a Nazi reception, which Goering was scheduled to attend, and smuggled in a pistol concealed in her handbag. For some reason Goering failed to appear and the opportunity was lost.)[5] Albert's contact and helper in Cologne at this time was Willy Huppertz, of the Free Workers' Union of Germany (FAUD), the clandestine German section of the AIT. Huppertz was a redoubtable figure, who helped rebuild the West German anarchist movement after 1945.

Having left school in 1937, Albert worked variously as a gas company clerk (he was sacked after a few months for union activities), on the tote at Hackney Wick greyhound stadium, as a brewer's clerk (for the J T Davis pub chain), a trainee reporter on the *Sunday Referee* (sacked again for his political activities, he 'got through Christmas that year quite well on a chance remark I heard in a pub about someone looking as if he needed Bob Martin's dog conditioner. I sold it to a dozen panto comics...'[6] It was the start of Albert's career as a joke writer), fairground promoter, theatre hand and warehouseman. Occasionally he worked as a film extra: he appeared briefly in Leslie Howard's *Pimpernel Smith* (1941), an anti-Nazi film that followed the line revolution, not victory, in Europe. The plot called for communist prisoners, but by the time the film came to be made Stalin had invaded Finland and the script was changed to anarchist prisoners. Howard insisted that real anarchists, including Albert, be used in the concentration camp scenes. One consequence of this meeting was Howard's introduction to Hilda Monte, which may have contributed to his death. Howard was en route to Lisbon to meet representatives of the German Resistance when his aeroplane was shot down.

Garrulous Good Soldier

IN 1939 Albert was one of the editors of the short-lived anarchist paper *Revolt!* and took part in an ill-fated attempt to organise an Anarchist Federation, but when war broke out, in September that year, the anarchist movement in Britain was woefully ill prepared to oppose it.

The general line, decided at a private meeting called by the veteran shop steward Tom Brown* (*see below*), which Albert attended, was of 'registering as conscientious objectors, making as defiant a statement of principles as possible, and then entering the armed forces.' While seeing this as 'the closest one could get to making a stand for one's principles without adopting the ultra pacifist stand which meant very little', Albert recognised that the position was not without shortcomings. In practice he favoured a more 'Schweikian' approach to answering the call-up, taking advantage of his notoriety in official circles as 'a red hot anarchist' to avoid war work: 'In my case and that of several others, though we were not exempted, the Ministry then refused to call us up. For four years of the war we were in this state of limbo. The Ministry of Labour was actually calling on me to register for other forms of civilian labour, which I declined, and when I spoke at meetings the police sometimes turned up and

---

*** Tom Brown (1900–1974) and the
Shop Stewards' Movement**

Tom had worked in engineering on Tyneside
during WWI. There he had taken part in the
huge self-organisation of workers at their places
of work, known for short as the shop stewards'
movement. This had been precipitated by the
betrayal of workers' rights by the labour leaders
in 1914 and the refusal of union membership to
multitudes of new women industrial workers. He
was to spend his life building democratic shop-
floor organisations, with all delegates mandated
and subject to instant recall. Tom took part in
numerous strikes and was the author of many
articles, on subjects varying from piecework to
the Peasants' Revolt. He also wrote several pamphlets, including *The British General Strike*,
What's Wrong with the Unions? and *Lenin and
Workers' Control*. The manuscript of his autobiography disappeared shortly before his death,
and is still missing.

---

demanded to see my identity card. When I produced it
I left them baffled.'[7]

In the meantime, with Tom Brown, Marie Louise
Berneri and Vernon Richards, Albert 'decided to publish a bulletin, *War Commentary*, as *Revolt!* had collapsed and we were all that remained of the production
team.'[8] The first issue of *War Commentary* appeared in
November 1939. From the beginning it took a strong
anti-war position, formulated by Albert as: 'War can be
ended by revolution, but no revolution can be won by
compromise with Imperialist War.'[9] Albert's articles for

War Commentary are models of revolutionary journalism, remarkable for their practical application of anarchist principles to the specific problem of advancing the revolution in wartime.[10] One particularly noteworthy article, that deserves to be reprinted in full, examined the military policies pursued by Germany and Britain ('*blitzkrieg*' and 'spontaneous defence'), and contrasted them with the revolutionary strategy and military policies of Marxists and anarchists, concluding that: 'anarchist revolutionary strategy cannot be based on national tactics, any more than national warfare can be based on guerrilla tactics. Armed insurrection without industrial action must fail. But industrial action without armed force to back it up has also failed... The policy to be adopted is one of liquidation of the barricades: revolutions cannot be fought side-by-side like nations against nations. They can only be fought by industrial action backed by military action – that is to say, without trenches, without planned boundary lines, certainly not by national ones.'[11] The anarchists in London addressed the problem of defence more directly later in the war, by acquiring and burying caches of military small arms, for use in the event of invasion or revolution.

A second Anarchist Federation, kept secret in case of repression, was formed at the Workers' Circle Hall, New Cavendish Street, on 28 April 1940, with Albert as its secretary. *War Commentary*, though nominally published by Freedom Press, became the new organisation's (unavowed) organ. The ambiguous standing of Albert's position with regard to the call-up allowed him to operate virtually full time on behalf of the new Federation, speaking at meetings across England, Wales and Scotland, in addition to writing for and editing *War Commentary*. Later in the war, he handed over the secretaryship of the Anarchist Federation to concentrate on editing (with Fay Stewart as secretary) *Workers in Uniform*, a bulletin circulated privately inside the armed forces, whose circulation climbed to 4,000 (twice as high as the open publication *War Commentary*): 'Our attitude to the Army... had been to agree that the way of the 'skyver' rather than the striker was to be recommended. Our ideal was the Good Soldier Schweik... We evolved a scheme whereby, by mere dumb helplessness on the part of the victim, it took the bureaucracy three years instead of three weeks to call a man up. Oddly, this appealed to far more people than did conscientious objection.'[12] Editorship of *Workers in Uniform* later passed to *War Commentary*'s cartoonist, John Olday* (*see below*) ('If, while I was editor, the bulletin's ideal was Schweik, it now became Spartacus. Olday insisted on the lessons of the German Revolution, and the discussion on tactics overflowed into *War Commentary*, with articles on the setting up of soldiers' councils.'[13]

Between 1941 and 1943, Albert worked in Blackpool for the comedian Roy Barbour, and was an active union organiser in the Variety Artistes' Federation. Returning to London in 1944, he was arrested in a theatrical agent's office in Regent Street as 'technically a deserter', for not responding to his call-up papers ('I had spent the larger part of the war arguing about why I hadn't any'[14]). Sentenced as a civilian to 21 days for 'non-reporting' and to a further six weeks for failing to notify a change of

***

* John Oldav

BORN in Germany of mixed Scottish-Canadian parentage, John Olday (Oldag) took part in the revolution in Germany in 1918, while still at school. The author of *The Kingdom of Rags* (1939) and *The March of Death* (1945), he emigrated to Australia after the war and dropped out of anarchist activity, being better known there as a gay rights activist and folksinger Olday returned to London in the early 1970s, but was snubbed by his former comrades at *Freedom*, and instead joined the *Black Flag* editorial group, as well as publishing his own idiosyncratic bulletin *Mit Teilung*.

***

address, Albert joined John Olday in Brixton prison. (Arrested for carrying a typewriter in the blackout, Olday received 12 months for possession of a false ID card, but his refusal to give evidence on his own behalf, or indeed to speak at all, landed him at the Old Bailey, where he was sentenced to two years for 'desertion'.

From Brixton, Albert and Olday were drafted into the Pioneer Corps and transferred separately to Prestatyn military prison in Wales, and from there to the notorious Stakehill military detention camp.

They were still there in February 1946, when the newly established anarchist paper *Freedom* (started after the police closed down *War Commentary* and arrested its editors) informed its readers:

'Another of our comrades who is a victim of ruling class discrimination is Albert Meltzer, also undergoing a sentence of detention on a technical charge of desertion.

Albert Meltzer is another militant who has been in the anarchist movement for the last ten years, and has shown a great activity in working for the working class cause against the imperialist deceptions of Tory and Labour politicians.'[15]

On Anarchist Secret Service

Shortly afterwards, Albert was shipped off to join a Pioneer Corps unit in Egypt, from where (as 'our man in the Middle East') he contributed a regular column for *Freedom*, 'Middle East Notes', in which he brilliantly analysed events in the region. In November 1946, Albert was one of the key figures (with the Irishmen 'Ginger' Foran and Mick O'Callaghan) in the famous 'Cairo Mutiny', when striking servicemen in the Canal Zone set up soldiers' councils that lasted for two months. Court martialed twice, Albert was eventually posted to a regular Pioneer Corps unit near Ismailia in 1947, before being shipped back to England and demobbed in Aldershot in 1948.

Back in 'civvy street', Albert found things very different from 1944. A Labour government, not armed revolution, had followed the end of the war. And the anarchist movement, too, had changed. The Anarchist Federation had split in 1944, and an influx of middle-class intellectuals and pacifists grouped around *Freedom* was casting its baleful influence far and wide. Years later, Albert admitted that he backed the wrong horse by siding with the would-be 'purists' against the anarcho-syndicalists when the Anarchist Federation split, and he regretted not having joined the Syndicalist Workers' Federation which broke away. It was the SWF's connection with the by then moribund AIT and the 'Intercontinental Secretariat' of the CNT in Toulouse, which obstructed the anti-Franco Resistance, that put Albert off. He only began to see the error of his ways in the 1960s, after he learnt of the participation of SWF members in the activities of the FIJL* (*see below*).

For the most part, the immediate post-war years through the 1950s until the mid-1960s were a bleak period for anarchist activity in England. Albert increasingly felt like The Last of The Mohicans as he watched the 'liars and liberals' (a term coined by Albert for the *Freedom* editors and a reference to a special issue of *Black Flag*) in charge of *Freedom* peddle their cosy notion of permanent protest, not class struggle, to a generation of intellectuals who believed revolution 'outdated'[16] Some people in the movement naively persisted in the belief that nothing had changed. But when Herbert Read accepted a knighthood for 'Services to Literature' in 1953, and the editors of *Freedom* offered apologies and explanations in print, it was too much for Albert's old Glasgow comrade Frank Leech he dropped dead of a heart attack, aged only 53.[17]

Albert largely kept himself apart from 'the movement' during this period, but even in these 'wilderness years' he never ceased activity entirely. With M. P. T. Acharya in Bombay, Albert set up the Asian Prisoners Aid Committee, edited with Albert Grace and the help

> ## FIJL – The Iberian Federation of Libertarian Youth
>
> Formed in 1932 as the youth wing of the Spanish anarchist movement (though its militants often retained their membership well into middle-age!). The FIJL was a principal target of the communist terror in Catalonia in May 1937. It later bore the brunt of the post-war resistance to Franco. In 1965 it broke with the MLE (Spanish Libertarian Movement in Exile) in frustration with the lack of support for the armed resistance.

of Philip Sansom *The Syndicalist* (May 1952 to April 1953), and took part in rent strikes of private tenants in the St. Pancras district of North London (1959–64). Also, with J. M. Alexander[18] and Kitty Lamb, he helped start the Radio Freedom League (1961), and contributed a stream of articles on anarchism and secularism to the *Rational Review* (1964) and *The Iconoclast* (1966).

While working briefly for Reuters in 1948, Albert went on holiday to Spain to renew old contacts, and was 'hooked into' the post-war anti-Franco Resistance. It was a time when the old 'gangs' that included comrades like the Sabaté brothers, Juan Busquets and Miguel García were being smashed, and the firing squad or long years in prison were the only rewards for resistance. Albert was not deterred. It was to provide a 'respectable' business front for the Spanish anarchist intelligence service that he opened offices at 374 Gray's Inn Road, London. A similar 'office' was established in Paris at the same time.

After the reorganisation of the Spanish Resistance in 1962, Albert's work for anarchist intelligence became more active, and in his autobiography he admitted: 'I became inextricably involved in what some of us termed the 'International Solidarity Movement' and others the 'First of May Group'. Later, in Brussels, it came together as the International Revolutionary Solidarity Movement (IRSM).[19]

Vernon Richards tried to poke fun at this intelligence work for the Spanish Resistance when it was mentioned in Stuart Christie's obituary of Albert[20], but whether he did so from ignorance, confusion, or just plain malice is not clear (he chose to remain silent when Albert mentioned it in his autobiography and was still alive to defend himself). Richards's attack in *Freedom* [21] gave the impression that Albert's resistance role took place during the Spanish Civil War, and so it couldn't have happened, instead of in the 1960s. But those in a position to know – in Barcelona the CNT and in Paris Octavio Alberola (for many years Franco's 'public enemy number one', as the comrade chiefly responsible for organising the armed resistance after 1961) have testified publicly to Albert's steadfastness and personal courage in carrying out clandestine work, inside and outside Spain.[22]

The restructuring of the Spanish Resistance on an international level in 1962 was instrumental in reviving anarchist movements throughout Western Europe and beyond.[23] The 'British connection' was first highlighted by the arrest of Stuart Christie in Madrid 1964, during an abortive attempt to assassinate the Spanish dictator.

Albert had barely met Stuart in 1964, and was not privy to his ill-fated mission: 'I did not know then how the FIJL had affected some of the new wave of members of the SWF and linked them with Spanish youth in France, whom I knew was inspiring growing determination for the Iberian Liberation Council (CIL).[24]

'One or two of them were only dabbling in politics but one, Stuart Christie, was in earnest'[25] Stuart's arrest marked a point of transition for Albert, from struggling on his own to support the Resistance ('usually when they were already on trial for their activities and some outside intervention was needed'), to participating in it fully.

On 30 April 1966, the ecclesiastical adviser at the Spanish Embassy in the Vatican, Monsignor Marcos Ussia, was kidnapped in Rome. The next day, at a clandestine press conference in Madrid, FIJL Secretary Luis Andres Edo announced that the action had been carried out by the First of May Group to focus attention on the plight of anarchist prisoners in Franco's gaols.

Among the group's demands was the release of three French anarchists – Alain Pecunia, Bernard Ferry and Guy Battoux (they were granted an official pardon a few weeks later) – and of Stuart Christie. A year later (April 1967), the First Secretary and Juridical Counsellor of the Spanish Embassy was abducted in London, an incident that has never been publicised. One of the proposals put to him was that if Christie was not released in the near future, 'they would initiate a campaign against the Francoist embassies and representatives all over the world'[26] After the machine-gunning of the private cars of two Spanish diplomats, and of the American Embassy in London on 21 August 1967, the Spanish Government took the hint. A month later Stuart Christie was released.

Albert has been criticised for being 'conspicuously absent from all attempts to help Stuart while he was in a Spanish prison'[27] (though the secretary of the Christie-Carballo Defence Committee, Mark Hendy, has pointed out that Albert invited them to use his Central London premises[28]). What his critics were not in a position to know was that behind the scenes Albert was part of the First of May Group's activities in London, which got Stuart out.

Raising the Black Flag

Albert was still very much a 'lone wolf' in 1964, when he accepted an invitation to speak at a meeting in London, where he first met Ted Kavanagh. Ted represented a new generation of activists, who owed nothing to the quietism of *Freedom*. Listening to Albert, Ted was 'amazed to hear anarchism described, for the first time so far as he was concerned, in terms of class struggle rather than liberal negativism and pacifism'. With Ted and some others, Albert 'formed a caucus within the newly formed London based groupings, then called London Anarchist Groups 1 and 2, roughly based on the divisions between supporters of FP and the SWF.'[29]

Together, the new team of Kavanagh-Meltzer also published and edited the satirical *Cuddon's*

Cosmopolitan Review (April 1965–67), named after Ambrose Cuddon, the first consciously anarchist publisher in England, who welcomed Bakunin to London in 1861. *Cuddon's* was very much of its time, mixing satire, humour and political commentary, but many of its articles would be worth reprinting today. Also members of the Cuddon's group were Anna Blume and Jim Duke, who started the 'Wooden Shoe' bookshop in New Compton Street. The Cuddon's group was also active in the national seamen's strike in 1966, publishing a strike bulletin, *Ludd* (the brainchild of Joe Thomas), which was edited by Albert, 'Digger' Walsh, and Albert Grace. Throughout this period (1963–1968), Albert earned a precarious living as a publisher and bookseller (at 283 Gray's Inn Road and 7 Coptic Street, and with Ted Kavanagh ran The Coptic Press in Pentonville Road), before joining *The Daily Sketch* as a copytaker in 1969, and later *The Daily Telegraph*.

After the return of Stuart Christie from Spain in 1967, the Cuddon's group became the nucleus of the Anarchist Black Cross, an idea first implemented by the Russian anarchists and revived by Albert, after he saw that Stuart's knowledge of Spanish prisons would make it possible to organise direct aid for imprisoned anti-Francoists. The Anarchist Black Cross very quickly turned the defence of class struggle prisoners into a springboard to action by others, and its work was immeasurably enhanced by the release of Miguel García from prison in Spain in March 1969. The presence in London of Miguel, a veteran of the 'old' Resistance who was determined to go on fighting, had a terrific impact on a generation of anarchists then turning to new forms of struggle.

Albert was incredibly active at this time. Besides earning a living, and his work for the Black Cross, he co-authored *The Floodgates of Anarchy* with Stuart Christie (published 1970), dashed off a constant stream of articles and pamphlets, and worked with Miguel over the summer of 1970 to produce *Franco's Prisoner* 'We wrote "Franco's Prisoner" together: he dictated in Spanish, I wrote it down in English, and we then went hammer-and-tongs for a week arguing and revising it.'[30] The book is arguably Albert's masterpiece.[31] Albert was also the driving force behind *Black Flag*, launched in 1970 when the *Bulletin of the Anarchist Black Cross* changed its name. From these modest but very practical endeavours came a new Anarchist International that defined its existence through activity, not organizational affiliation.

The work of the Anarchist Black Cross made it the target for intense police reaction, including the murder of three of its Secretaries – Giuseppe Pinelli (Milan, 15 December, 1969), Georg Von Rauch (West Berlin, 4 December 1971 and Tommy Weissbecker (Augsburg, 2 March 1972) and the arrest again of Stuart Christie in London, on charges connected with the 'Angry Brigade'.

Two comrades accused of involvement with the 'Angry Brigade', Jake Prescott and Ian Purdie, were already awaiting trial in London in 1971 when MLN 'Tupamaros' guerrillas, fighting against the military dictatorship in Uruguay, kidnapped the British

Ambassador in Montevideo, [Sir] Geoffrey Jackson, demanding the release of MLN members held by the regime. The guerrillas asked Miguel García to publicise the case in London, and Stuart Christie thought the Black Cross could help: 'Albert was particularly enthusiastic about it. He felt it showed we could help prisoners far from our own point of view, and we might incidentally get them to throw in as brokerage Purdie and Prescott against whom there was little evidence.'[32]

Albert's idea was for Miguel García and Antonio de Figueredo (a former Portuguese diplomat, active in the anti-Franco Resistance) to act as go-betweens, which could lead to Jackson's immediate release, in return for the release of Prescott and Purdie. Stuart approached two Fleet Street journalists known for their connections with the Foreign Office, who expressed interest in the idea, but the only immediate result was his arrest the next day on charges connected with the 'Angry Brigade' (the police planted detonators in the car he was driving – Albert's!). But a month later, 100 MLN prisoners, including Raul Sendic and Julio Marenales Sanz (whose release had been specifically demanded), escaped from the heavily guarded Punta Carrera prison, and three days later Geoffrey Jackson was set free.

Thus, in August 1971, Stuart joined seven other comrades in prison, and spent sixteen months awaiting or on trial of the 'Stoke Newington Eight' before being acquitted of all charges and released in December 1972* (*see below*). In his absence, Albert and

The 'Angry Brigade' Trials

THE trial of Ian Purdie and Jake Prescott ended in December 1971. Ian was acquitted of all charges, and Jake convicted on the flimsy evidence of having admitted to addressing two envelopes that contained 'Angry Brigade' communiqués. He was sentenced to fifteen years, reduced to ten on appeal, for 'conspiracy to cause explosions'. The Stoke Newington Eight case (30 May-6 December, 1972) was the second of two 'Angry Brigade' trials, and ended with the acquittal of four of the eight defendants. The other four, Hillary Creek, Anna Mendelson, John Barker and Jim Greenfield, were all sentenced to ten years for 'conspiracy to cause explosions'. No one has ever been convicted of any explosion claimed by the 'Angry Brigade'. Until the recent 'McLibel' case of Dave Morris and Helen Steel, it was the longest trial in British legal history

Miguel edited *Black Flag* and opened the Centro Ibérico/International Libertarian Centre (first in Gilbert Place in Central London, and then in a basement in Haverstock Hill, Hampstead) as a meeting place for anti-Franco activists and anarchists from all over the world. The 'Centro' has subsequently passed into international anarchist folklore as the birthplace of so many of the campaigns and groupings that left their mark on the 1970s.

The most embarrassing aspect of the SN8 trial for Albert as he later was to recall was his being called upon to give evidence, as a witness for the prosecution!

'Doyen of the Anarchist Movement'

THE 'Angry Brigade' trials were still going on in London, while a new campaign of armed struggle was getting under way in Catalonia.

The Iberian Liberation Movement (MIL-GAC, December 1971–1974) was a fighting organisation of anarchists and 'council communists' that had grown out of the strike movement in the Spanish car industry. Their 'Autonomous Combat Groups' robbed banks to finance anti-Franco propaganda and operated with swashbuckling audacity. On one occasion, when the police confiscated a MIL printing press, the MIL simply seized the police station and took the press back again!

Most of the members of the MIL were frequent visitors to London and to the Centro Ibérico, and Miguel García worked closely with them. One in particular, Salvador Puig Antich, was well known here. He lived with Albert and Miguel in Finsbury Park (in the 'almost historic' 123 Upper Tollington Park, North London), and accompanied them on a speaking tour of England. Shortly afterwards, Salvador returned to Barcelona and was arrested in a shoot-out with police on 22 September 1973. Despite widespread protests, Puig Antich was sentenced to death and garroted at dawn on 2 March 1974. His death provoked a wave of action all over Europe (including a march to the Spanish Embassy in London, and the bombing of the Spanish Cultural Institute in Dublin). [33]

In Paris, the Groups of International Revolutionary Action (GARI) kidnapped a Spanish Banker,

Balthasar Suarez (3 May, 1974), demanding the release of 100 political prisoners in Spain and the repayment of some of the CNT funds seized by Franco. Suarez was released unharmed after payment of an undisclosed sum, but French police arrested nine anarchists in Paris and accompanied Scotland Yard Special Branch officers on raids in London, and a *Time Out* journalist who had covered the story, David May, was threatened with prosecution for not revealing how he came into possession of Suarez's driving licence.

The campaign of solidarity with the MIL and GARI, which in England was chiefly waged by Albert and Miguel, brought many comrades new to the movement into active contact with the Spanish Resistance, and helped to inspire a number of affinity groupings to engage in direct action themselves. Among those who were part of this solidarity movement was a group of anarchists in Dublin who were sentenced to various prison terms in 1974. Two of them, Noel and Marie Murray, went on the run and were not recaptured until 9 October 1975. Sentenced to death by hanging, for the shooting of a policeman following a bank raid, the Murrays were only saved by a massive campaign of international solidarity. The Murray Defence Campaign was actually initiated by Miguel García (Albert was in Spain when news of the death sentences came through), but it was Albert who became the most tireless figure in it,[34] and he continued to struggle on the Murrays' behalf long after the 'campaign' was over.

The Murrays' case was probably the most dramatic of many campaigns in which Albert was tireless. His association with comrades who were active in armed struggle groups during the 1970s has often resulted in Albert being cast in the role of an anarchist 'Godfather' figure (usually benevolent, sometimes sinister[35]), which continued after his death.

In fact, Albert was more usually the last to know what his comrades were up to, and he was all too frequently the target of unwanted police attention as a result. But that never stopped him from doing all he could to raise support and solidarity for those engaged in acts of derring-do after they landed in prison.

Police fears of a 'new Angry Brigade' culminated in the 1979 'Persons Unknown' trial, at which Albert was called to testify for the defence. Two of those brought to the Old Bailey on this occasion were members of the *Black Flag* editorial team, Iris Mills and Ronan Bennett. The police had a score to settle with Ronan after he was acquitted of the killing of a police inspector in Belfast and was released from Long Kesh Prison. First they arrested Ronan and Iris in Huddersfield (March 1977) under the Prevention of Terrorism Act, and issued an Exclusion Order against him. When that failed, they arrested them again (24 May 1978), in London, on trumped-up charges of conspiring with 'persons unknown' to cause explosions, later reduced to robbery charges. In the Huddersfield raid, a Special Branch man had referred to Albert as the 'doyen of the anarchist movement'. When the 'Persons Unknown' case came to trial in 1979[36], Albert turned in such an impressive performance in the Witness box that a defence solicitor commented that he reminded her of Alec Guinness!

The police also made strenuous efforts to establish a link between those arrests and an earlier case involving Dave Campbell, Brian Gibbons and myself, jokingly referred to by Albert as the 'Lewisham Three'.[37]

In his memoirs, Albert commented: 'On this occasion the police were not able to make a political issue out of it, although they dropped asides around the court about their links with the Murray Defence Campaign and hinted before the trial about the accused 'preparing to finance a new Angry Brigade'.[38]

Memorial

The death of Miguel García in December 1981 hit Albert hard. They had worked closely together since Miguel's release in 1969, and were surely one of the great double-acts of revolutionary history (more Laurel and Hardy than Marx and Engels, but no less effective for that!). And the stories of their car journeys around Europe (west *and* east) are the stuff that legends are made of. We published a memorial publication, *Miguel García's Story*, bringing together appreciations of Miguel with the 'missing' chapters from *Franco's Prisoner* and Albert's contributions to it are gems of his writing at its best. Albert spoke at Miguel's funeral in North London, and the only time I have seen him as deeply affected by someone's death was in 1990, at the funeral of Leo Rosser.[39]

After the collapse of the Autonomy Club (a promising but short-lived project begun by Iris Mills and Ronan Bennett in 1981 and the death of Miguel, Albert concentrated his energies on keeping *Black Flag* going, and building up the Direct Action Movement (formed in 1979, as the British section of the IWA), which Albert saw as the realisation of decades of effort and propaganda aimed at creating a viable organisation of class struggle anarchists. He was active throughout the miners' and printers' strikes of the 1980s. And even after he retired from the print industry in September 1987 he continued to take a full part in the activities of the DAM (which more recently changed its name to the Solidarity Federation). Though in the last years of his life he was increasingly critical of developments within the CNT (he told me that coming into money, as a result of winning the 'patrimony' case against the Spanish Government, was the worst disaster that could befall the CNT), and of the return of narrow and bureaucratic attitudes within the IWA, Albert never wavered in his belief that anarchism could only become a reality through the working class organising itself along anarcho-syndicalist lines.

Albert's refusal to accept or collaborate with the elitist pacifists and liberals who sought to reinvent anarchism in their own image after WWII, and his scepticism of the New Left in the 1960s earned him a reputation for 'sectarianism'. Paradoxically, it was the discovery of class struggle anarchism through the 'sectarianism' of *Black Flag* under Albert's editorship that convinced so many anarchists of my own and subsequent generations to become active in the movement. And it was to deny the liberal 'objective' academics a monopoly over anarchist history that Albert founded the Kate Sharpley

Library, and helped to turn it into the most comprehensive anarchist archive in Britain (except, no doubt, the Special Branch's). If Albert were to be remembered only for his contribution to the Spanish struggle (about which several volumes could easily be filled), he would have earned his place in revolutionary history and the hearts of anarchists. That he contributed so much more, in so many different fields of struggle, and over such a long period of time, is truly remarkable.

Happily, he lived to see the publication of his autobiography *I Couldn't Paint Golden Angels*, a unique account of working class rebellion. At the time of his death, he was full of plans for the future, concerned as ever about helping imprisoned comrades (he was busy trying to raise support for Jean Weir in Italy[40]), and eager to explore the possibilities of the Internet.

That he suffered his fatal stroke while attending a conference of the Solidarity Federation is testimony in itself to Albert's determination never to quit. His close friend and comrade Stuart Christie, looking back on thirty years activity alongside the inscrutable Albert, recalled: 'He often seemed like a member of a tug-of-war team; you never quite knew if he was there to make up the numbers or as the anchor of the operation.'[41] Now that he is no longer there at all, the gap is immense.

Ros Wynne-Jones, commenting on Albert's funeral in the *Independent on Sunday*, wrote: 'In the death of Albert Isidore Meltzer...the international anarchist movement proved it was still vividly alive.'[42] That that is so is perhaps Albert's finest memorial.

NOTES

1. Meltzer, *I Couldn't Paint Golden Angels*, p. 88.
2. See 'A Rebel Spirit', *KSL Bulletin* No.4 (1994) and No.5 (1995).
3. Albert wrote two, conflicting, accounts of this gun-running operation. The first (*The Anarchists in London 1935–1955*, published in 1976 and also available in Kindle) gives the major role to Alf Rosenbaum, and omits White's involvement, leaving the impression that White only came onto the scene later when he returned from Spain. The second account (*I Couldn't Paint Golden Angels*, pp. 57–8) restores the detail of White's participation. Gerald Howson, author of *Arms for Spain* (published in 1998 by John Murray Ltd), in a letter to Stuart Christie, thinks Albert's account relates to the following incident: 'In September 1936 a small cargo steamer, *The Bramhill* (1,834 Tons GR) belonging to Angel-Dalling & Co of Cardiff, carried about 820 tons of rifles, machine guns and ammunition from Hamburg to Alicante, where she arrived on 1 October, and that the crates were labelled for delivery to the CNT. The shipping agent was the Lessen Aktiongesellschaft of Hamburg, Cologne and Lübek. *HMS Woolwich*, in harbour at the time, radioed the information to London within hours. The Foreign Office believed that the German government "must have been completely taken", as had the Foreign Office itself, which had approved the insurance by Lloyds of the shipment in the belief that it was going to Saudi Arabia and Yemen. The FO must have contacted the German embassy immediately, for within a day or two the Germans explained that the arms were not German but Czechoslovakian, that they had been sent by a Swiss businessman to Hamburg, via Zurich and Cologne, before the outbreak of the fighting in Spain and had been stored there after his customer had been unable to pay for them. It then reminded the Foreign Office rather stiffly that Hamburg was a Free Port where the German government had no powers to prevent the transit of arms from anywhere to anywhere. The matter was then dropped and forgotten...

'For reasons too complicated to go into here, I suspect that *The Bramhill* was allowed to leave on the authority of Canaris, the chief of Abwehr counterintelligence, who foresaw an eventual clash between the anarchists and the Communists and calculated that a limited shipment of arms to the CNT would help to push things in the desired direction, especially when it became known, as it did, that the arms had come from Nazi Germany. Other cargoes of arms for the Republicans left Hamburg and they were all skillful acts of betrayal. There was a ring of five arms-traders in Berlin, Liège and London who knew very well how to manage these things.'

4. 'Schwarzrot' (Black & Red) was an affinity group formed by German seamen who jumped ship in Glasgow (where they were helped by Billy Campbell's old mentor Frank Leech) before moving to Birmingham to attract less attention. Also involved with the group was Ernst Schneider, a veteran of the German naval mutinies of 1918, who (as 'Icarus') wrote *The Wilhelmshaven Revolt*, republished by Simian Press in 1975 (and also now available on Kindle).

5. The story of the anarchist assassination attempt on Goering, which to the best of my knowledge has never been published, was told to me in 1976 by Hilda Monte's 'husband' John Olday (who was involved on the periphery of these activities).

6. Meltzer. *I Couldn't Paint Golden Angels*. p. 56.

7. *Ibid*. p. 84.

8. *Ibid*. p. 84.

9. Meltzer. "How Will the War End?' *War Commentary* Vol. 1/No. 2. December 1939.

10. See especially, Meltzer, 'Anarcho-Syndicalism – an outline of constructive Anarchism' *War Commentary*, Vol. 1/No. 6. April 1940.

11. Meltzer, 'Military Policy', *War Commentary*, Vol. 2/No. 8. June 1941.

12. Meltzer, *The Anarchists in London 1935–1955* (Cienfuegos Press. 1976 p. 13 and Kindle, 2013).

13. *Ibid*., p. 27 Olday died in highly tragic circumstances in 1977 aged 72.

14. Meltzer, *I Couldn't Paint Golden Angels*. p. 99

15. *Freedom*, 23/2/46.

16. One of the editors of' *Freedom* at the time, attacking Albert, was reported thus: "'I don't know what he ever did but make a noise," said Charles Crute of the Freedom Press. "He was into revolution – rather an old fashioned concept of anarchism. We regard him as a romantic.'" – "Anarchy reigns as a comrade is remembered", *The Daily Telegraph*, 29/11/96.

17. See: Meltzer, 'Frank Leech', *The Syndicalist*, Vol. 1/No. 10, February 1953, and *I Couldn't Paint Golden Angels*, p. 126.

18. James Alexander was murdered in his sleep on 24 August 1993, aged 84 years, by a burglar who fled to Poland. An Australian-born 'writer' Owen Davis, was later brought back from Warsaw (where he had written a novel, entitled *Murder*, in which he described how he killed Alexander) and sentenced to life imprisonment. The case provided Albert with one of his last campaigns against bureaucracy, after Camden Council kept the body for over a year awaiting autopsy, and gave away Alexander's personal archive and unpublished manuscripts to the Marx Memorial Library! See: interview with Albert by Craig Kenny, 'Murder victim's amazing life' *Camden New Journal*, 3/2/94; Mike Verdin, 'Funeral for murder victim' and 'Life for writer who described murder in novel', *Ham & High Express*, 21/7/95; also *Black Flag* No. 203 Autumn 1993, and No. 205 Autumn 1994.

19. Meltzer, *I Couldn't Paint Golden Angels*, p. 210–211.

20. Christie, 'Anarchy's torchbearer' *The Guardian*, 8/5/96.

21. Vernon Richards, 'Instead of an Obituary' *Freedom*, Vol. 57/No. 10, 18/5/96.

22. See the testimonials to Albert's work for the Spanish Resistance on following pages.

23. A recent polemical survey of the International Workers Association (AIT/IWA) noted: 'The IWA suffered post-war stagnation – the CNT was in exile; the Swedish SAC was sucked into collaboration with the state in order to survive in a society dominated by social democracy, robbing the international of its last mass organisation; prominent anarcho-syndicalists like Rudolf Rocker and Agustin Souchy

came out in favour of bourgeois democracy. Resistance continued in Spain, however, and provided a focus for networks of anarchists in Western Europe.

'When younger revolutionaries attracted to resistance became active in the late '60s and the '70s as part of the re-emergence of revolutionary activity characterised by workers militancy in Britain and the "events" of 1968, a link with our history was there. Our comrade Albert Meltzer played a key role in this process, and *Black Flag* is part of its legacy.

'With the death of Franco in 1975, underground networks of anarcho-syndicalism, as well as participating in armed resistance actions (both branded "terrorism" by the state), re-formed the CNT. The reaction of the exiled organisation is instructive they denounced the militants for using the name CNT, as it was the property of the exile organisation!

'Reality won through eventually, and led to the revival of the IWA in the late '70s...' (Peter Principle, 'What is Anarcho-Syndicalism?', *Black Flag* No. 211, May 1997).

24. Iberian Liberation Council (CIL) formed by the FIJL in December 1962 to co-ordinate the armed resistance to Franco.
25. Meltzer, *I Couldn't Paint Golden Angels*, p. 161.
26. Stuart Christie, *The Christie File* (Partisan Press, 1980), p. 105.
27. John Pilgrim, 'Correcting Christie', *Freedom*, Vol. 57 No. 11, 8/6/96.
28. Mark Hendy, 'The Christie-Carballo Committee and the rewriting of history', *Black Flag* No. 209, October 1996.
29. Meltzer, *I Couldn't Paint Golden Angels*, p.145.
30. Meltzer, *Miguel García's Story* (Miguel García Memorial Committee & Cienfuegos Press, 1982), p. 54.
31. Miguel García, *Franco's Prisoner* (Rupert Hart-Davis, 1972). Long since out of print and now a collector's item (but now available on Kindle).
32. Christie, *The Christie File*, p. 257
33. Besides Puig Antich, two other members of the Centro Ibérico met violent deaths: Robert Touati (a French com-

rade accused of belonging to the GARI), blown-up with Juan Duran Escribano in Toulouse 8/9 March 1976; and Oriol Sole Sugranyes (MIL), shot dead escaping from Segovia Prison, 9 April 1976. Another close comrade of Albert and Miguel's from the 'old' Resistance, Laureano Cerrada Santos, was shot dead by a Spanish police agent in Paris on 18 October 1976.

34. It is only fair to acknowledge here the very active role played in the Murray Defence Campaign by Miriam Daly of the IRSP (Irish Republican Socialist Party), who was shot dead in her Belfast home by a Loyalist death squad (who first tied her up and tortured her).

35. Connor Brady, *The Irish Times* 10/12/76), accused the Anarchist Black Cross (and by association Albert) of corrupting the 'idealism' of Noel Murray, and asked rhetorically who put guns in his hands and taught him to shoot. More recently, Nicolas Walter has claimed that Albert was 'involved in the turn towards urban guerrilla methods which appealed to frustrated revolutionaries and culminated in this country in the Angry Brigade in the 1970s' Walter, 'Albert Meltzer' *The Independent*, 10/5/96.

36. Arraigned with Iris and Ronan (on various charges relating to a series of raids for arms and money between 1 January and 21 May 1978) were Vince Stevenson, Trevor Dawton, Dafydd Ladd and Stewart Carr. Ladd jumped bail and failed to appear for trial; he surrendered to police three years later and was convicted and sentenced to nine years on other charges. Carr, an unstable criminal associate of Ladd's and an outsider to anarchism, pleaded guilty to anything the police put to him and was sentenced to nine years. All the others were acquitted.

37. 'The Lewisham Three' – so called because they were arrested in Lewisham, South London, on 5 October 1977, during a raid on Mecca bookmakers. All three received seven years imprisonment. As Albert joked, 'the bookie always wins'!

38. 'The sham-ans in the peace and flowers movement were indignant with "Black Flag". The funniest comment passed on to me was that our collective was trying to start, in imita-

tion of the Campaign for Real Ale, a campaign for Real War, and that Phil Ruff was in jail for armed robbery "and he's only the cartoonist". Presumably the lay-out team laid out the corpses' Meltzer, *I Couldn't Paint Golden Angels*, p. 278.

39. Leo Rosser (30 July 1964–24 March 1990). A very active member of DAM-IWA, the Anarchist Black Cross and *Black Flag* in the 1980s, Leo conducted valuable 'investigative research' into international fascism, before succumbing to severe depression and committing suicide.

40. Anarchist publisher Jean Weir (*Bratach Dubh*, Elephant Editions, *Insurrection*, *Anarchismo*) was in prison in Italy (together with a number of Italian and Greek comrades), serving a sentence for armed robbery. For background to the case see: 'Trials and Tribulations in Trento' *Black Flag*, No 206, 1995, 'In the Frame in Italy', *Black Flag* No 207 1996; and *The Grand Guignol Frame-up against Anarchism has Materialised*, October, 1996 (BM Ignition, London, WCIN 3XX).

41. Christie, 'Anarchy's Torchbearer' *The Guardian*, 8/5/96.

42. Ros Wynne-Jones, 'After the Anarchy, the Comedy', *The Independent on Sunday*, 26/5/96.

**Albert Meltzer, anarchist; born London, 7 January
1920; died, Weston-Super-Mare, North Somerset,
7 May 1996**

What follows is the complete original text of the
edited obituaries that appeared in *The Guardian*, 8
May, *The Daily Telegraph*, 11 May and *The Times*, 15
May 1996.

ALBERT MELTZER was one of the most enduring and
respected torchbearers of the international anarchist
movement in the second half of the twentieth century.

His sixty-year commitment to the vision and
practice of anarchism survived both the collapse of
the Revolution and Civil War in Spain and the Second
World War; he helped fuel the libertarian impetus of
the 1960s and 1970s and steer it through the reactionary challenges of the Thatcherite 1980s and post-
Cold War 1990s.

Fortunately, before he died, Albert managed to
finish his autobiography, *I Couldn't Paint Golden
Angels*, a pungent, no-punches pulled Schweikian

account of a radical twentieth century enemy of humbug and injustice.

A lifelong trade union activist, he fought Moseley's Blackshirts in the Battle of Cable Street, played an active role in supporting the anarchist communes and militias in the Spanish Revolution and the prewar German anti-Nazi resistance, was a key player in the Cairo Mutiny during the Second World War, helped rebuild the post-war anti-Franco resistance in Spain and the international anarchist movement. His achievements include *Cuddon's Cosmopolitan Review*, an occasional satirical review first published in 1965 and named after Ambrose Cuddon, possibly the first conscious anarchist publisher in the modern sense; the founding of the Anarchist Black Cross, a prisoner's aid and ginger group and the paper which grew out of it – *Black Flag*!

However, perhaps Albert's most enduring legacy is the Kate Sharpley Library, probably the most comprehensive anarchist archive in Britain.

Born in 1920 into a mixed marriage in the London of Orwell's *Down and Out...* in which there were few homes for heroes, but many heroes fit only for homes, Albert was soon enrolled into political life as a private in the awkward squad. His decision to go down the road of revolutionary politics came, he claimed, in 1935, at the age of 15 as a direct result of taking boxing lessons. Boxing was considered a 'common' sport, frowned upon by the governors of his Edmonton school and the prospective Labour MP for the area, the virulently anti-boxing Dr. Edith Summerskill. Perhaps it was the boxer's legs and footwork he acquired as a youth that gave him his lifelong ability to bear his considerable bulk. It certainly induced a lifetime's habit of shrewd assessment of his own and opponents respective strengths and weaknesses.

The streetwise, pugilistic but bookish schoolboy attended his first anarchist meeting in 1935 where he first drew attention to himself by contradicting the speaker, Emma Goldman, by his defence of boxing. He soon made friends with the ageing anarchist militants of a previous generation and became a regular and dynamic participant in public meetings.

The anarchist-led resistance to the Franco uprising in Spain in 1936 gave a major boost to the movement in Britain and Albert's activities ranged from organising solidarity appeals, to producing propaganda, working with Captain J R White to organise illegal arms shipments from Hamburg to the CNT in Spain and acting as a contact for the Spanish anarchist intelligence services in Britain.

Albert's early working career ranged from fairground promoter, a theatre-hand and occasional film extra. Albert appeared briefly in Leslie Howard's *Pimpernel Smith*, an anti-Nazi film that did not follow the line of victory but rather of revolution in Europe. The plot called for communist prisoners, but by the time Howard came to make it, in 1940, Stalin had invaded Finland, and the script was changed to anarchist prisoners. Howard decided that none of the actors playing the anarchists seemed real and insisted on real anarchists, including Albert, be used as extras in the concentration camp scenes.

One consequence of this meeting was Howard's introduction to Hilda Monte, a prominent but unsung hero of the German anarchist resistance to Hitler, which may have contributed to his subsequent death en route to Lisbon.

Albert's latter working years were spent mainly as a second-hand bookseller and, finally, as a Fleet Street copytaker. His last employer was, strangely enough, *The Daily Telegraph.*

While by nature a remarkable gentle, generous and gracious soul, Albert's championship of anarchism as a revolutionary working class movement brought him into direct and sustained conflict with the neo-liberals who came to dominate the movement in the 1940s.

Just as people are drawn to totalitarian movements like fascism and communism because of their implicit violence and ideological certainties, many otherwise politically incompatible people were drawn to anarchism because of its militant tolerance. Albert was vehemently opposed to the re-packaging of and marketing of anarchism as a broad church for academe-oriented quietists and single-issue pressure groups. It was ironical that one of this group, the late Professor George Woodcock, should publicly dismiss anarchism as a spent historical force in 1962, blissfully unaware of the post-Butskellite storm which was about to break and the influence anarchist and libertarian ideas would have on this and generations yet to come.

It was his championship of class-struggle anarchism, coupled with his scepticism of the student-led New Left in the 1960s that earned Albert his reputation for sectarianism. Paradoxically, as friend and *Black Flag* cartoonist Phil Ruff points out in his introduction to Albert's autobiography, it was the discovery of class struggle anarchism through the 'sectarianism' of *Black Flag* under Albert's editorship that convinced so many anarchists of his and subsequent generations to become active in the movement. The dynamic and logic of Albert's so-called 'sectarianism' continued to bring countless young people into the anarchist movement then and for a further thirty years until his untimely stroke in April 1996.

It is difficult to write a public appreciation of such an inscrutably private man. Albert Meltzer seemed often like a member of a tug-of-war team; you never quite knew if he was there simply to make up numbers or if he was the anchor-man of the whole operation.

To Albert, all privilege was the enemy of human freedom; not just the privileges of capitalists, kings, bureaucrats and politicians, but also the petty aspirations of opportunists and careerists among the rebels themselves.

Much of what he contributed to the lives of those who knew him must go unrecorded, but he will be remembered and talked about fondly for many years to come by those of us whose lives he touched.

Stuart Christie

Last Words
by Stuart Christie

**Lewisham Crematorium,
Friday 24 May 1996, 12.55 p.m.**

'Fellow friends, comrades and colleagues of Albert.

'I am under sealed posthumous instructions from the benign man himself not to be maudlin, mock heroic or engage in sloganeering of any type – otherwise, like Freddie Kruger, he'll be back, probably to Angel Alley.

'Suffice it to say that Albert Meltzer was – to all who knew him – apart from a handful of mean-spirited and unlamentable nonentities – universally respected and loved, across the generations and continents, as a man of profound humanity and generosity of spirit whose words and writings wrought flames in other men's hearts; a man who dedicated his life to turning today's dream into tomorrow's reality.

'Albert's familiar figure may no longer be with us in body, but as long as we carry our pleasant memories of him in our hearts and, most importantly, continue to talk about him – Albert's cheery presence will neither fade nor die.

'I'd like to make my farewell to Albert with W. Johnson Cory's translation of a poem by the pre-Christian Greek epigrammatist Callimachus in tribute to his teacher, mentor and friend Heraclitus.

They told me, Heraclitus, they told me you were dead;
They brought me bitter news to hear and bitter tears to shed;
I wept, as I remembered, how often you and I
Had tired the sun with talking, and sent him down the sky.

And now that thou art lying, my dear old Carian guest,
A handful of grey ashes, long, long ago at rest,
Still are thy pleasant voices, thy nightingales, awake;
For Death, he taketh all away, but them he cannot take.

Salud, amigo!
Salud, compañero!

Commemorating Albert Meltzer.
(Communiqué delivered by a representative sent by the CNT/AIT Regional Committee of Catalonia to the funeral of Albert Meltzer)

These lines are intended to bear witness to our heartfelt tribute to the memory of our comrade Albert Meltzer.

The career of Albert – committed from his youth to the struggle in defence of Ideas – was especially marked by his unfailing and direct support for the resistance activity of the CNT against the Francoist dictatorship. This was demonstrated by his personal involvement, with other British comrades, in the underground struggle against the regime. He risked his own liberty in delicate intelligence missions and in militant organisational liaison inside Spain during the Dictatorship, which is yet another reason to attend this meeting in commemoration of Albert Meltzer, whose record embodies the highest measure of human solidarity.

Barcelona, May 23, 1996
CNT Regional Committee, Catalonia
Barcelona Local Union Federation
Editorial staff of *Solidaridad Obrera*
Foundation of Libertarian and Anarcho-syndicalist Studies

'I'll be back for May Day in Las Cocheras.' That was how Albert Meltzer said goodbye on his last visit to Barcelona. He was returning to London to put the finishing touches to his autobiography '*I Couldn't Paint Golden Angels – Sixty Years of Commonplace Life and Anarchist Agitation*'. He was also going home much preoccupied with the international situation, what with the rise of fascism and more especially by the frictions within the IWA at a time when more cohesion was what was required.

There was nothing out of the ordinary about his 'I'll be back'. He had said it literally dozens of times, in the underground days, during the period of transition. Albert always 'came back' literally or figuratively, always available and always ready to help out. Hamburg, Paris, Brussels, Madrid or Barcelona's Barrio Chino – it was all the same to him. His comradely heart was as big and startling as his wits were quick.

Albert's activism started as a 15-year-old in London and he very soon came into contact with the Spanish revolution and the CNT-FAI Aid Committees sponsored by Emma Goldman (along with Berneri's daughter, Marie Louise, her husband, Vernon Riccione [Recchioni], the anarcho-syndicalist Tom Brown and the novelist Ethel Mannin, all revolving around the newspaper *Spain and the World*). From then on he had a particular empathy with the Spanish militant anarchist movement that was to endure right up to his death this year. But he was to become alienated from the British group that carried on with *War Commentary* and *Freedom*.

Albert, for all the time he was committed to the revolutionary struggle against Franco, was also intensely active in London. He lived through the defeat of revolutionary Spain, the Second World War and the bleak years of squabbling and heated controversies. Underneath the easy-going surface Albert was an incorrigible enthusiast and he made himself enemies with more than one outburst on more than one occasion. Yet he knew the ins-and-outs of the London and British movement with all its leftist sub-fauna better than anyone. With that special zeal, sometimes dubbed sectarian, he was able to motivate the younger and more radical elements. It was not all sweetness and light – there was no way he could have painted those golden angels.

The '60s and '70s saw an upsurge in the anti-Franco struggle and of British activism. These were the years of the First of May Group, the launching of *Black Flag* the Anarchist Black Cross, the Angry Brigade and, in partnership with Miguel García, of the Centro Ibérico, through which widest spectrum of exiles passed – and of Cienfuegos Press. Albert was never far away, despite that 'generation gap.'

Dear old Albert, many a year has passed since those coffee shops in the middle of Soho in the 1950s... and come what may, London and the British movement are not going to be the same again now that you have left them, never to return.

Postscript: The Windmills Strike Back
by 'Acrata'

Vile is the vengeance on the ashes cold;
And envy base to barke at sleeping fame
—Spenser *Faerie Queene*, Bk. 2 c. 8

For over fifty years, the publishers of the fortnightly magazine *Freedom* have tried to be the cuckoo in the nest of the anarchist struggle in Britain. Year in, year out, for decade after decade, Freedom Press has gobbled up the donations of well-wishers, dissipated the energies of activists, and concealed or denounced the efforts of those engaged in the fight against class oppression.

When the lengthy and positive obituaries of Albert appeared in newspapers in Britain and abroad, to be followed by equally long accounts of his funeral and of his political legacy, the gentlemen of Freedom Press, with a lack of grace unusual even for them, gave vent to almost apoplectic rage.

The most poisonous article was entitled 'Instead of an Obituary' and appeared in *Freedom* on 13 May 1996. In it the author, Vernon Richards, rejoiced over the death of his one-time comrade and attempted to cast doubt on Albert's sixty years of unstinting commitment and militancy. Richards described Stuart Christie's widely published obituary of Albert as 'fantastic' and its author as an 'erstwhile amateur "terrorist" anarchist'.

At the very least, appearing only seven days after Albert's death, Richards's article was insensitive towards those who were attempting to come to terms with the thought of life without their friend and comrade and his many virtues, not least his staunchness, good cheer and wit. At worst, Richards's abuse of Albert and his memory was an attack on the very cause to which he devoted his adult life.

Frenzy

The reasons for such frenzy are not difficult to see. First of all, anarchism as a cause can flourish very well without *Freedom*, but *Freedom* can only continue its wretched, half-baked existence if it never has to confront any challenge from committed militancy, either directly or by comparison. In life, Albert was foremost among those who personify such a challenge, and was more than a match for the Freedom Press group, who have been trying for several decades to reduce the anarchist movement to their own uninvolved, cynical, manipulative, non-campaigning, decayed and enfeebled versions of stateless socialism and resistance to social injustice. In Albert's death, however, these poseurs of pseudo-revolt saw an opportunity to defend their position by delivering personal attacks on their principal critic.

Second, it hardly needs to be pointed out that the vindictive pursuit of the departed, the insult to the grief of those who mourn, the abuse of the fondest and most cherished memories of the man and his works – these are not the doings of even half-decent people. They are the wretched utterances of those who can no longer even contemplate in others the vision, the will and the courage that they themselves have lost, and which they most certainly are unable to do anything to regain. Just as a drunk will compensate for his own inadequacies by turning to the bottle, to see himself as the better of anyone else in the world, so those who have given in to cynicism, disillusion and despair seek to cover their own shame and misery by defiling the life or memory of anyone who aspired, hoped and struggled to the last.

Self-serving

The self-serving, jaundiced abuse of Albert's memory by Richards and his associates, the rush to revile one whose life was well and wisely led, were therefore largely unsurprising, though they were not, in their unintended humour, without their lighter moments. (Albeit that in themselves these moments were reminders of matters that are perhaps less amusing). The most obvious instance is the description, quoted above, of Stuart Christie as an 'amateur terrorist': presumably, in the pecking order of the world Richards inhabits, professional terrorists have a higher rating! (Though if we consider that the most professional terrorist of all is the dictator, then this can only confirm still further the worst suspicions aroused by Richards' remote and autocratic control of Freedom Press, over several decades!)

Some months after Albert's death, the cudgels of Freedom Press were taken up by one of its old associates – Richard Boston, a freelance journalist interested in writing and broadcasting about anarchism, or, more particularly, anarchists, since the early sixties. The interest of the national press in anarchism, stimulated by Albert's funeral, provided Boston with the opportunity for a major commission on the subject, and a chance for the Freedom Press group to pour further scorn upon Albert's career and character, for the purposes already discussed above.

The means chosen by Boston to further secure *Freedom's* pre-eminence (in the eyes of the Freedom Press group, if nowhere else) was a longish, eight-page article in the 'Weekend' supplement to *The Guardian* of 16 November 1996, entitled 'Anarchy Among the Anarchists'. Despite the length of the piece, and the rather amusing elevation to the anarchist pantheon of the litigious litterateur Oscar Wilde and the town-planner Colin Ward (an admirer of Milton Keynes), one half of the piece was a self-congratulatory public relations exercise on behalf of Freedom Press, lacking in accuracy, originality, inspiration or insight. Anarchism was presented historically and politically as a ragbag of dotty if charming ideas produced by a number of eccentric outcasts from the privileged classes. Nowhere was it mentioned the work of activists throughout the country who have been striving to put anarchist ideals into practice – the '1-in-12 Club', Bradford, the 'Norwich Solidarity Centre' the 'Red and Black Club' Sheffield and many others. These people are the ones involved in the cutting edge of anarchism, both at work and socially, and have done more for anarchism than the countless issues of *Freedom* that have presented anarchism as an intellectual ideal rather than the concrete challenge to the corruption of capitalism which it is. Those around *Freedom* and by extension, Boston, know nothing about grass-roots anarchist activism in the UK.

Furious Abuse

The other half of the article was aimed at piling further abuse on Albert's memory. The level of Boston's journalistic professionalism and bias can be gauged from the following extraordinary anecdote: 'At the Anarchist Bookfair in October, Stuart Christie was sitting at a stall in one corner of Conway hall diametrically opposite the *Freedom* stand. There were rumours that friends of the late Albert were planning some direct action, such as turning over the *Freedom* bookstall but in fact nothing untoward occurred.'

For the record, Stuart Christie was not at the Bookfair, nor has he attended one for many years; nor did Boston make any attempt to contact him to confirm the above story or to check any of the facts or prejudices expressed in his article.

The article did, however, provoke disgust among many anarchists who were appalled at its blatant repetition of Richards' malicious and envious tirade of abuse against Albert. We do not know how many wrote to *The Guardian Weekend* to complain about the Boston article, but the editor chose only to publish two, at least one of which was heavily cut.

Octavio Alberola, the coordinator of all the Spanish Libertarian Movement's (MLE) who organised international and internal anti-Franco resistance in the 1960s wrote a detailed rebuttal of Vernon Richards' lies about Albert's role in the anti-Franco resistance which we reproduce here, in full.

To: The Editor, *The Guardian Weekend*

From: Octavio Alberola
Paris, 20 November 1996

I was appalled to read the disgraceful and unjustified attack on the memory of the late Albert Meltzer in *The Guardian Weekend*, Saturday 16 November, in what passes as an overview of anarchism.

I first came into contact with Albert during the early Sixties in my role as coordinator of the Defensa Interior (DI) committee. The DI was the secret committee set up in early 1962 by the Second Intercontinental Congress of the Spanish Libertarian Movement in Exile (MLE: the National Confederation of Labour [CNT], the Iberian Anarchist Federation [FAI], and Iberian Federation of Libertarian Youth [FIJL]), to organise and co-ordinate all clandestine activities against the Francoist regime, in particular, preparing attempts on the life of the dictator General Franco.

I do not wish to engage in polemic; I should simply like to place on record the fact that Albert Meltzer, who worked with us throughout the period, was a brave and selfless supporter of the anti-Francoist movement during the long years of repression, who regularly gave freely of his time, money and, on occasion, risked his freedom – and perhaps even his life – on compromising trips into Spain on behalf of the libertarian anti-Francoist movement. My view of Albert is shared by many of the surviving older generation of anarchists involved in the Spanish Civil war, and in the subsequent guerrilla war against Franco from 1939 to the mid-1950s. Albert Meltzer was always prepared to put his time, money, resources and his freedom wherever he thought it would be helpful for others.

I am one of those who respected Albert Meltzer, and in the same way you have published such false information, I hope you will publish the contrary opinion about Albert Meltzer, at least in respect to those of your readers who deserve the complete and true information.

Yours faithfully
Octavio Alberola
(Coordinator, Defensa Interior, MLE, 1962–1963)

The final word should be the following hitherto unpublished letter to *The Guardian Weekend* from

Mark Hendy, an anarcho-syndicalist activist in the 1960s who was a friend of Albert's and the Secretary of the 'Christie-Carballo Defence Committee' set up in August 1964.

To: The Editor, *The Guardian Weekend*
From: Mark Hendy, Devon, 20 November 1996

Lonely dogs often bark the loudest, and the vehement criticisms of Albert Meltzer which Richard Boston (16 November) makes so much of come from persons with little or no significance in anarchism today.

If Albert had a fault beyond his exceptional kindness, generosity and humour, it was his Quixotic tendency to invest with life and importance opponents who were actually inert, moribund or marginal. Only in this sense does he deserve the splenetic obituaries – they are the windmills striking back!

Mark Hendy

In Memory of Albert
by Simon McKeown

Simon McKeown, close friend and confidante of Albert (and co-executor of Albert's will, with Stuart Christie) adds his personal memories and thoughts on his friend.

At the time of Albert's death I could not really express the regret and the massive sense of loss that affected me. We became close friends following the death of our joint friend Leo Rosser. As Leo had kept an eye on Albert in practical ways in his lifetime, I picked up Leo's mantle, and soon both myself and Albert became good friends. During the next 14 years we talked of many things, we did lots, and by and large we laughed.

It would be easy to read about the politics of Albert's life and to gain little sense that he existed as an ordinary, happy person. He existed in other areas outside of politics and interacted with non-political people the world over. His interests were wide and varied, and his knowledge, often combined with experience was vast. He loved history and languages, learning Swedish a few years before he died. He had the capacity to bring unusual and mostly very funny tales to any discussion and he could relate life experiences to his own and those with him. Somehow he often made things better, he made them make sense – a common sense mostly – at least for me. Through him I have heard tales of Florence Nightingale, of the army, of exiles, cultures, languages, the circus and even strawberry-picking with the last man hanged in England.

His life story was a mixture of joy, sadness, but always humour. He grew up in the music halls of Hackney, and one of my later musical experiences with Albert involved us watching some old time stuff, Albert singing along with such a broad smile. He was a shy person, and talked little of the two women he lost in his early life. He never really got over those losses and spent much of his older life living alone – technically speaking of course. There are literally countless visitors from around the world, who have enjoyed Albert's hospitality, settee, floor, bed, in London over the past 30–40 years. If he had a home its door was always open. His openness was never tainted by the bitterness which so often taints those involved in politics for a lifetime. He had a sense of life. He enjoyed it for its worth.

Broadwater Farm was still a farm when he was a child. He wasn't interested in either the Catholic or Jewish influences in his background. Tottenham was the nearest football club to him as a child. His father at the time knew several players and they were often round his house. The next time he had any interaction with football was when we went, completely out of the blue to see Leyton Orient some 55 years later. We went to a pub near Walthamstow Marshes, and Albert asked the landlord whether he was still barred. Banned as he had been some 55 years earlier!

Besides football we visited castles, nature reserves, childhood seaside resorts, and so much more. One of the highlights of these trips was a visit to the 1-in-12 Club in Bradford where a band played Marlene Dietrich songs for him. They have now established The Meltzer Library in his memory.

Before he died we discussed death, and what he thought about it. He felt calm about it somehow, and we often joked that when he was a hundred we'd get him on the TV refusing his letter from the Queen, doing a 'Kate Sharpley.'

Albert was considering moving out of London before he died, and I am sad that my good friend is not around the corner from me. However, that is not to say that he needed his eyes broadening out of London. He was widely travelled. It was my privilege to visit a few European cities with him and it is to my regret that we never travelled together more.

His death in a seaside resort was fitting, as they were among his favourite places. He dreaded being a burden, yet had been burdened by many others all his life. He died well looked after in a dignified pleasant hospital which is more than some can ask. He exemplified dignity and human kindness even at this stage, unlike those who sought to darken his memory after his death.

He was saddened to see the problems affecting the CNT, but buoyed by his visits to Scandinavia, He still had so many avenues of interest, both inside and outside of politics to explore and before his death he was becoming an adept user of the Internet. Aged 75 he was still happily able to dismiss NF/BNP threats on his life, with the reply, 'It's quite a while since I hit a fascist'.

I find it hard to dismiss the disgusting attacks on Albert after his death, when so many where still suffering shock and in mourning made by people who patently never knew him. Albert would have quickly suggested that we forget them and as they struggle with their own bitterness and lies and in turn die I feel I agree. They are not worth remembering. They are not worth a jot.

That so many young people came to pay tribute to him at his funeral was testament to his ability to bridge communication gaps, to provide insights, knowledge and experience and in general be a friend to so many.

Let us therefore never forget our friend Albert Isidore Meltzer, whose humour, dignity, kindness, and trust, which were so clearly visible to all.

Albert Meltzer at the typewriter
(Source: Phil Ruff)

Leah Feldman on leaving Russia
(Source: Kate Sharpley Library)

Albert Meltzer 17 April 1939
(Source: Phil Ruff)

Soldiers in Cairo (Source: Phil Ruff)

Above: Albert standing next to his bookshop in King's Cross,
283 Gray's Inn Road, London (Source: Phil Ruff)

Below left: Octavio Alberola (Source: Stuart Christie)
Below right: Albert October 1962 (Source: Phil Ruff)

Stuart Christie, London, 1968
(Source: Stuart Christie)

Stuart Christie and Albert Meltzer,
outside the Queen's Head pub,
Crouch End Broadway, 1968
(By: Ken Sutherland
Source: Stuart Chistie)

The Cuddons Gang, Brighton, October 1969. Left to right: Ted Kavanagh, Albert Meltzer, Arthur Moyse, Jim Dukes (Source: Phil Ruff)

Giuseppe Pinelli, Milan Secretary of the Anarchist Black Cross, murdered December 1969 (Source: Stuart Christie)

Miguel García, Placa de St. Felip Neri, Barcelona, 1979
(Source: Stuart Christie)

John Olday performing cabaret at the Centro Iberico, London, 1974
(Source: Stuart Christie)

Salvador Puig Antich, garrotted, March 2, 1974
(Source: Stuart Christie)

Albert Meltzer & Stuart Christie, Conway Hall,
London 1975 (Source: Phil Ruff)

Philip Sansom, Miguel García and Albert Meltzer, Conway Hall 1976
(Source: Phil Ruff)

Ronan Bennett and Iris Mills a few days prior to the "Persons Unknown"
trial at the Old Bailey at a "Friends of Cienfuegos Press" social at the
Conway Hall, London, September 1979 (Source: Stuart Christie)

Albert Meltzer & Stuart Christie, Birmingham 1981
(Source: Phil Ruff)

Albert with the author and *Black Flag* cartoonist, Phil Ruff,
London 1984 (Source: Phil Ruff)

Funeral Procession of Albert Meltzer, Lewisham, London, 24 May 1996

(Source: Stuart Christie)

Funeral Procession of Albert Meltzer, Lewisham, London, 24 May 1996

(Source: Stuart Christie)

Part of the press response to Albert Meltzer's funeral (Source: Stuart Christie)

scene outside the crematorium in Lewisham, south London, yesterday

After the anarchy, the con

The funeral of a veteran anarchist last week turned into a rare revolutionary celebration. **Ros Wynne-Jones** reports

AT a crematorium in the heart of suburbia last week, a crowd of 200 people from around the world gathered to celebrate the death of an anarchist. A stand-up comedian told jokes in the assembled mourners until they were rolling in the aisles; a home video showed the deceased himself laughing and he had to mop his streaming face; the coffin slid away to a crackling recording of Marlene Dietrich. Earlier, in a procession led by two plumed horses and a jazz band, friends denounced the dead man's detractors. In the death of Albert Isaac Meltzer, who died last week aged 76, the international anarchist movement proved it was still vividly alive.

There was nothing out-of-the-still about Friday's funeral, but then there was nothing ordinary about the life of Albert Meltzer. He became an anarchist in 1935, at the age of 15, and over the next 60 years became a key player in the international anarchist movement. He was a veteran of the battle of Cable Street against Oswald Mosley, the Spanish Revolution, anti-Nazi resistance in pre-war Germany, and anti-Franco resistance in post-war Spain. He died in much the same spirit, after collapsing at an anarcho-syndicalist conference earlier this month.

Albert Meltzer was never very far from the barricades in life and, almost predictably, his death has produced a skirmish in the modern anarchist movement. Begun in the 18th Century by Marx's follower Mikhail Bakunin, it holds that people can live better without government, and has been at the forefront of much revolutionary action around the world.

One side holds he was the "torch-bearer" of international anarchism, the other that he was "sham" Vernon Richards, who over 50 years ago replaced with Meltzer the cantankerous objector at a Labour Exchange, is now among his fiercest critics. Last week the front page of the anarchist fortnightly, *Freedom*, carried a vitriolic attack on Meltzer by Richards, entitled "instead of an Obituary." "I believe that for the past 30

day. "But it takes all sorts to make a revolution."

Stuart Christie, who was with Albert Meltzer when he died and is the executor of his will, dismissed the article as "playing on Meltzer's grave." "It is polemic politness and poison from *Freedom*," he said "They are just a small group of revolu...

already the co-author of *The Floodgates of Anarchy* with Albert Meltzer, 36-year-old Christie was arrested in Britain as a suspected terrorist. He spent 14 months in prison on remand but was acquitted after the jury found the police had manufactured political evidence in his case.

As Albert Meltzer's literary executor, Christie is now inextricably linked to his long-time friend and collaborator. Commentators at the time of his celebrated trial recall that Christie also decide what anarchism is in 1996,

Anarchy's torchbearer

ALBERT Meltzer, who has died aged 76, was a torchbearer for the international anarchist movement. His 60-year commitment survived the collapse of the Spanish revolution, the civil war and the cold world war. He fuelled a libertarian impetus of the 60s and 1990s and stirred it enough the reactionary elements of the 1980s and 1990s.

Albert Meltzer's irrepressible verve was undimmed. He remained a light Mosley's blackshirts finely...

ALBERT MELTZER

Albert Meltzer anarchist
died on May 5 aged 76.
He was born on January
7, 1920.

CONVINCED that all privilege was the enemy of freedom, Albert Meltzer devoted his life to ideas struggle and libertarian revolution. For 60 years he was a standard-bearer for the international anarchist movement, rebelling not only against the principles of monarchy and capitalism, politicians and bureaucrats, but also against the petty, opportunist politicians which sprung up amid revolutionaries themselves.

His 60-year commitment to anarchism remained solid through all the vagaries and battles of the movement's history. He fought Oswald Mosley's blackshirts in Cable Street in 1936, he supported the anarchist resistance during the Spanish Revolution and championed anti-Nazi resistance efforts in pre-war Germany. During the 1990s revival of anarchism he fought off a neoliberal moderation of anarchist philosophy through his strict ideals, which was keen to renounce creative young people to become active revolutionaries themselves.

He occasionally even worked as an extra in films, taking the part of an anarchist prisoner in Leslie Howard's anti-Nazi film *Pimpernel Smith* (1941). Howard had insisted he take the role of authenticity real anarchists should be used to play the concentration camps scenes. However, it was one of his schoolboy experiences which was first to steer him towards the far Left,

where his chief ambitions were always to remain.

As Leytown Meltzer learnt learnt to ride, though the sport was an "unknown" by the school governors and especially by the prospective Labour MP. At the age of just 15, attending his first anarchist meeting, he found himself sparring in an intellectual arena when he defended his sport against the disperser of the movement. Emma Goldman. He became from then on a dynamic participant at anarchist gatherings, mixing general far left organisations and contributing to a

small but steady number of magazines. During the rise of Fascism in Spain, Meltzer came a vigorous supporter of the revolution in 1936, even as a mere 16-year-old. He committed himself to organise or solidify but also became a member of the anarchist movement. Towards the end of the 1940s Meltzer found himself working in Barcelona where he spent a large part of the decade with Capital White in organising arms shipments bombbung to Spain as well as a contact for the anarchist intelligence in Britain. After the war the revolution he had rebuilt in London in Spain.

During the Second World War Meltzer moved conscripted, registering conscientious objection however, he did serve Army and played a part Cairo Mutiny of 1946. Towards the end 1949, Meltzer found himself in a tradition of the war tinged redemptions of Left. At this time a new trend of thought was rising to dominate the anarchist movement. Meltzer as in his militant has, a sceptates convinced the schism should a...

And when I die, don't send me flowers

... Just ask what the boys in the back room will have — and let's all have a good laugh.

Gary Younge on an anarchist's last rites

"TO FOLLOW Albert Meltzer, one of the most cherished figureheads of anarchist movement, to final resting place yesterday, you need only have followed the black and red stars raised for roads from the scene of his funeral Colonial Cafe to the local crematorium in suburban south London, listening in the rain, they sit proudly on the lapels earlobes of the mourners, as black and with pacifistic a plenty, who brushed the finer to walk behind the ordinary funeral procession to the sounds of the Bill Jazz Southern Stompers Jazz.

By Dietrich's slate, *The Boys In The Will Have.*

Then came a: They Called his Campbell, folks minute video showed Meltzer overcoming an temper in him The stripping out, led by the the crematorium reduced to tears then that bid bade "If it were should be demonstrative company and there ear," for to

In the end the weary at the climbed into coaches and was the an different renwmbryant"

But in they I must to the it been so remoist Whilst remoist in his soul.

He wrote: "If someone and a God, or like poverty someone feeling for him nobody he was. In heaven the law. And if he wants to?"

movement led to conflict with the neo-liberals who dominated the movement in the late 1940s. Many otherwise leftist young people were drawn to anarchism intolerance. Albert was vehemently opposed to the re-packaging of anarchism as a broad church for academic-oriented guitarists and single-issue pressure groups. It was his championship of class struggle anarchism, coupled with the scepticism about the student-led New Left in the 1960s, which earned Albert his reputation for sectarianism.

Paradoxically, as friend and Black Flag co-founder Phil Ruff points out in his introduction to Albert's autobiography, *I Couldn't Paint Golden Angels*, it was the distinctive contribution to the renewal of class war anarchism in post-war Britain that earned Albert the respect he deserved. A revolutionary tradition in a satirical magazine to publication in 1986, and the founding of the Anarchist Black Cross, a prisoners' aid of direct action and the inaugural paper Black Flag. Born into the London of Cable Street and Oswald Mosley's fascist gary is Britain's most com-

Anarchy reigns as a comrade is remembered

By Sandra Barwick

THE anarchist movement is disunited even in death, as the events following the funeral of Albert Isidore Meltzer, anarchist and former Daily Telegraph copytaker, demonstrate.

Since his death at 76 in May, his brother anarchists have been squabbling about his role in history, with accusations that he exaggerated his exploits and libelled his comrades.

Mr Meltzer, who had, as he scented, a funeral with a jazz band and a stand-up comedian, disliked the *Freedom* Press and its editor and for years in his anarchist paper Black Flag, calling it liberal and pacifist.

He had described in his books how he fought Mosley's blackshirts in the Cable Street confrontation in 1936 and his involvement in the Cairo mutiny of 1946.

On his death, *Freedom* ran a piece called "In place of an obituary" saying that in his autobiography his accounts of events had "begun confusing the Cairo events. And made clear

Albert Meltzer was an international anarchist who often wrote a high-flown biography. Albert said he was 75.

Mr. Meltzer was the author of many articles and pamphlets, and was recognised by historians for

at the Anarchist Book Fair, in which Meltzer refused to shake hands with him. Mr Richards concluded "I believe that for the past 30 years he has done more than good to the anarchist cause..."

Fellow anarchists quizzed Meltzer about his combative stance upon the use of violence. With his pall of *The Daily Telegraph*, which he served for 36 years as a copytaker, there was sense being that of a mere warrior who pursued his love of violence only by proxy by Emma Goldman of the movement, pursued as if through an address of direct action Pierre-Joseph Proudhon, who sought the supremacy prosperity in itself.

"I don't know what he ever did not quite a write." said Charles Crane, of the *Freedom Press*. "He was his revolution — rather an old-fashioned concept of anarchism. He struggled with his old band commitment for a long time.

Friends of Mr Meltzer have defended his role. Stuart Christie, Meltzer's co-author and executor of his will, said at his funeral that the anarchist was "the arch sort there

jor source for scholars.

Mr Meltzer was born in London and trained as a boxer in his youth. He first became known in the anarchist movement when he argued with the famous radical leader Emma Goldman, who condemned boxing.

He smuggled weapons and served as an intelligence agent for the Spanish anarchists during the 1936-30 civil war in Spain.

He also worked as a movie ex-

a living as a bookseller and publisher, taking a less direct part in politics, but he ended his working life as a copytaker on Conservative newspapers — first the *Daily Sketch* and then the *Daily Telegraph*.

Meltzer returned to die an anarchic movement during the revival of the 1980s. He broke with the moderate associated with the established *Freedom Press*, whom he described as academics and masochistic and denounced as liberals and pacifists (even "non-violent fas-

Albert Meltzer

Albert Meltzer was active in the libertarian left for more than 60 years — he began assuming an anarchic meetings when he was 15, and died after collapsing at an anarcho-syndicalist conference when he was 76. He saw himself as a protagonist of the militant working-class anarchist movement, something which had existed in many parts of the world when he began but which scarcely exists anywhere today.

Meltzer was born into a Jewish family in Hackney. His father followed several trades — window-, tailo-, salesman — an encounter for of life. He won governor who but his school educated at well as the several suppor, aborn in where had pay to fro the anarchist downed and Proudhon and pacifists - "non-violent fas

He produced many articles, mostly in his own magazines.

Anarchy reigns at the swingin

AN anarchist is dead in his life. Albert Meltzer arranged for his funeral yesterday to be celebrated with crowd of about 200 was accompanied representative of a single revolutionary movement by the sound of Marlene Dietrich, though the close the Southern Syncopated Jazz Band.

Ending on a jovial note: Albert Meltzer's final journey had a jazz band, comedian, and the sound of Marlene Dietrich, though the c...

By Sandra Barwick

APPENDICES TO THE SECOND EDITION

1. Joint Manifesto of the Revolutionary Youth Federation and the Committees for Workers' Control

1) An Anarchist is a person who is opposed to governmental Society.

2) Since governments exist to protect property the Anarchists have evolved the theory of Anarchist Communism, which is not based on Property, and holds that all wealth be held in common by the community through the local "communes" (councils) wherein each works according to ability, and takes according to need. There would be no state. The communes would be linked by a free federation, and harmony of interest; would be maintained by mutual aid and agreement.

3) This is a philosophy of the future and its realisation demands a transitional stage which, logically, must be also libertarian, anti-State- and federal: the only such system at present is Revolutionary Syndicalism, recognised by Anarchists as a means to an end.

4) Revolutionary Syndicalism (Anarcho-Syndicalism) is the system of workers' unity in economic organisation fighting for immediate reforms under capitalism with the object of workers' control, following the abolition of the State after the Social General Strike or Revolution. Each branch of economic life would be run by the workers in that branch, operating through their Syndicalist Unions (Syndicates) without any State or political intervention – the mines to the miners, the factories to the factory-workers, etc. Social life would be run by the communes, which would consist of the local federation of all the syndicates. The national federation of all the syndicates would run international trade relations: the national federation of each syndicate would run their own national industry. The government of men would be replaced by the management of things.

5) The anarchist would, before the Revolution, prevent the domination of the syndicalist unions by parliamentarians and politicians and, after the Revolution, continue spreading the ideals of liberty so that the non-anarchist majority would dwindle to a minority and perhaps disappear, not through coercion (which would go with the State) but by moral persuasion as well as the practical results of collectivised life.

6) The immediate creation of a dual anarchist and syndicalist organisation is therefore obviously desirable, and we call upon the workers of Britain to form, unite

in and develop an Anarcho-Syndicalist body of labour unions, an anarchist federation and a revolutionary youth movement, in order that the struggle for freedom and socialism may recommence in the birthplace of free socialism in no uncertain fashion.

A.M.

From: *Revolutionary Youth Federation Monthly Bulletin*, Vol. 1, no. 1, 1st February 1938

2. Editorial
Makhno's "Black Cross"

It is fifty years since Nestor Makhno organised units of the Black Cross, originally intended as field-working units similar to those of the Red Cross (as used elsewhere in Russia, described in this issue). The Black Cross units in various cities of the Ukraine were for purposes of workers' self-defence, as well as for purely "ambulance" type activity. The use of Cossacks, the prevalence of White Guards, pogromists, as well as the growing Red Army, made it necessary for city dwellers to be able to protect themselves in the streets.

They wore no particular uniform except that, to enable themselves to be recognised at times of violence in the streets, they wore denim overalls with a recognisable armband. Their job was to organise resistance to sudden pogroms, whether the conventional Czarist pogrom, or the sudden onslaught of Red or White Guards.

Those who think of movements for self-defence purely in terms that we think of them in the West today (largely legalistic, like the Council for Civil Liberties, excellent though such a body is for its specific function) will find it surprising that a body organised solely for defence of prisoners, and for the protection of workers in their homes and factories, should have become one of the major adjuncts to the fighting forces of Makhno's peasant army. It was, indeed, the first urban army to be formed in the Ukraine; by 1920, when the Whites were an organised body aided by foreign intervention, the city-Makhnovistas, the Black Cross, was the only force in the towns that could organise military self-defence along with the peasants. They faced three enemies, Petliura in the West, the Bolsheviks in the North, and the monarchists in the East and South. But they were able to defend the cities though they were never a mobile force like the peasant army.

Most certainly, in a revolutionary situation such as existed in Germany when the Nazis were rising to power, it is highly necessary to have a movement that is able to resist. The mere provocation of the State by protest, when one can only be crushed by the full powers at the disposal of the State, is not enough. It is necessary, when fighting dictatorship, to be able to oppose a monolithic force to it that can fight back when attacked.

The Ukrainian "Black Cross" arose out of purely defensive needs, in order to protect workers occupying their places of work, to defend demonstrations in the streets, and so on. Its form of organisation might have been that of the Red Cross (even that of the Salvation Army, as one observer sneered!) but it was able to adapt that form of organisation into a fighting force.

"And Kropotkin said that in his view, the Royal Lifeboat Institution and the International Red Cross were examples of Mutual Aid, and presumably, of Anarchism!"

So runs the gentle joke of many a don commenting on Kropotkin's teachings. And he omits to point out that in the very same paragraph that Kropotkin says this, he grants the fact that "princes of the blood" and others have conferred their patronage on such organisations, after they have shown that they are socially acceptable, but that the actual work done by the lifeboatmen or the Red Cross volunteers is a supreme example of the principle of Mutual Aid between mankind. The lifeboatman does not count the profit; he does not argue with the sinking captain for commercial advantage (though he could, and capitalist morality would justify his doing so?).

The RED CROSS founded by Dunant has saved innumerable lives in warfare between nations. We are far from criticising it; but depending as it does on governmental tolerance, it has its limitations. It can arbitrate as regards the sick and wounded and imprisoned of, say, Germany and England; it cannot help those of Russia and Japan because the governments of those countries do not care a damn about their subjects and (at least in the Second World War) were beyond the point where they need care for public opinion. (Even the Germans would have protested had the Nazis left German POWs to their fate; but the Samurais of Nippon and the Soviet regarded them as "traitors".)

In the same way, it was always impossible to ask the Red Cross to look after the sick and wounded and imprisoned of the Class War. In a Civil War (e.g. Spain

1936) they might do so; but not in cases where there was no declared civil war. This gap in the Red Cross became particularly noticeable in Czarist Russia. The rulers of that country had in effect declared a civil war against their own subjects. In particular they used the Cossacks to murder the Jews. The Jewish population was a hostage to the revolution. If the Russian workers protested, the Czar diverted their revolutionary aims by organising a pogrom. It was at once an example to the Russian masses, and a warning as to what would happen to those who incurred official displeasure. When the "Black Hundreds" raided the Jewish districts, the police stood by. If ever the Jews resisted (and Anarchists and Bundists at times organised Self Defence Committees that fought back) the police stepped in and fought the defenders, arresting them for violent activity.

International Jewry organised its own committees for relief of the Russian Jews; but such bodies did not extend their help to the Anarchists and Bundists who had — dreadful to relate to the bourgeois sponsors of such committees — had the temerity to fight back. So a committee was formed in America, amongst Russian Jewish workers in particular, called the WORKERS RED CROSS (which changed its title after a few months to ANARCHIST RED CROSS, since the Red Cross Workers, asked them to do so to avoid confusion).

The ANARCHIST RED CROSS, centred in Chicago, raised a large amount of aid not only for the Jewish fighters in Russia but also for the entire Russian revolutionary movement. It sent field workers to Russian prisons, aided deportees and (not being bound by any convention such as the official Red Cross) also sent in illegal propaganda. The existence of such a body meant, too, that aid could speedily be sent to victims of the class war in many countries. Perhaps one day the full story of the Anarchist Red Cross will be told. (Its work was carried on for a long time after its demise by the Free Society Group of Chicago; in particular, comrades Boris Yelensky and Celia Goldberg.)

When the Russian Revolution came, the Anarchists needed their Red Cross units more than ever. The organisation set up, in many ways a continuation of the old A.R.C., was known as the Black Cross (partly to distinguish itself from the Bolshevik "Red" and partly again to save the Geneva organisation, doing good work in general relief, from embarrassment).

The Anarchist Black Cross was overwhelmed with work. The prisoners multiplied; there was no abatement in government tyranny. Alexander Berkman, expelled from Russia to Berlin, tried to cope with the fund for Russian prisoners, when a new demand came in (for the victims of the *Fascisti* in Italy). The album of Kropotkin's funeral (the last permitted non-Bolshevik demonstration in Russia, for which Anarchists were especially released from Russian jails, which we may at some time reproduce) was sold to alleviate distress amongst prisoners in Italy and Russia. With repression in Spain, the rise of the Nazis, and depression in the countries from which the money was coming, the Black Cross collapsed.

There were similar organisations from time to time (e.g. *Solidaridad Internacional Antifascista*, whose secretary in London was Ethel Mannin) which did good work in their time. When, however, our friend Stuart Christie was arrested in Spain, we found the lack of any organisation which could help in such a case. In particular, Amnesty did not want to know. They were prepared to take up the cases of political prisoners provided those prisoners were "innocent", their ideal prisoner was a University professor charged with liberal thinking, who had never lifted a finger against repression in his life and had still found himself in jail.

Many comrades from many countries sent food parcels and the like to Stuart; from Germany and elsewhere, people who had never met him. (And this gave us particular satisfaction, remembering 1945, when we had organised sending food parcels to Germany, which had come from Britain, USA and even Palestine; a factor helpful in keeping many old militants alive in the post-war period.)

In prison, the Anarchists and some other political prisoners (but not the Moscow-liners, who refused to collaborate) had formed a commune in which they shared their food parcels from outside. Spanish prisons permit food and medical supplies to be sent from outside; if one relied on the prison hospital one would die neglected. But, while parsimonious, it is prepared (unlike British jails) to allow donations from outside. When Stuart returned, he knew who was in difficulties in Spain, he was indeed a "mouthpiece" of the libertarian political prisoners in Spain.

We began to send parcels, and in doing so, revived the idea of the ANARCHIST BLACK CROSS.

Some start has been made to making it a permanent organisation.

It is not intended to be a charity.

It is to organise solidarity for victims of the class war.

We are sending food parcels at present but by no means wish to limit what we send (whether to Spain or elsewhere?) merely to food or medical supplies, vital as these are to those concerned. If the governments would recognise our work, we would confine it to humanitarian purposes and relief of prisoners.

As it is, we deem it part of our task to help with other facets of the struggle; in places where we can provide effective solidarity.

In some parts of the world Anarchists are able to work without undue interruption by authoritarian forces; and they can also be isolated geographically from participating in the more active struggle such as exists in Spain.

Their aid is needed. We hope to bridge the gap.

A. Meltzer

Bulletin of the Anarchist Black Cross vol.1, no.1
(July 19, 1968)

3. A sense of Freedom

The following was found on Albert Meltzer's computer after his death. Though possibly unfinished, it can be taken as his parting words to the editors of *Freedom*.

The proprietor of *Freedom* is always reluctant to discuss how it is run, how he got and has retained unbroken control for over 50 years, what this status is exactly, how he is planning for it to be controlled after his death and on what basis it claims to an unbroken line of succession since 1886. Or even if he believes in Anarchism. His indignation over my autobiography was always predictable.

The present editors, subject to recall by "the Boss" (as he is called behind his back), did not see how they could avoid reviewing my book, particularly as some unsuspecting readers had sent in flattering reviews. The task was given to Nicolas Walter, anxious to rebut his double dealings described in the book.

Following his exposure in *Black Flag* regarding his collaboration with the late H. Montgomery Hyde, Tory Unionist MP, former Intelligence officer and later writer, Walter wrote, in a private letter to myself, declaring that this was far worse than anything he had ever said about me (true!) and if I denied it (though fully attested) and restrained *Black Flag* from referring to the matter again (beyond my remit anyway) he would apologise for all the lies he told about me in *Freedom* and elsewhere. I would not agree and the lies continue (I do not know how many as I gave up reading it). Unlike the Nazi C18 [Combat 18], who received an invitation to explain themselves after they torched the premises, I, it seemed, had no "right to reply" to the lies in that journal, formerly the property of the movement. (Unless, perhaps, I put on a swastika and burned the place down).

The ageist sneer "Uncle" is rich coming from a journal whose principals are ten years older than myself, who have been dribbling in their bibs for decades, and written by someone slowly dying in a wheelchair. Alternatively, it might just refer to the pathetic attempts at fantasy satire written by Labour Party/Freedom Press/Winchester School parasite Arthur Moyse some 20 years ago, thus suggesting that his dreamed up characters with names of his acquaintances had some basis in fact, in lieu of anything worse he could dig up.

I pass over the alleged factual inaccuracies as Nicolas Ridicolas does not dare say what they were but promised to reveal them in secret etc. to select readers. The "false and furious" attacks are presumably on himself. Though he dares use the term "evasive", the real objection is that I have revealed too much that Richards and Walter want kept secret.

Usually the allegation is that I have a personal vendetta against FP or some of its bosses. This is to obscure the fact of the real political differences which all real anarchists hold. "Emotional instability" is a new twist in the paper war against me. It was last alleged against one of its voluntary contributors (suspended but since permitted to resume) for daring to suggest they give practical help to squatters.

The curious remark about the attacks on "anyone and anything to do with Freedom Press" suggests that anyone other than the few living off it are nothing. Long term neglect[ed figures] and even founders are rescued from deliberate neglect and even shameful treatment by the new "officials". Are George Cores, Tom Brown, Leah Feldman, Ambrose Barker, Kitty Lamb, Guy Aldred, Frank Leech, Matt Kavanagh, Hilda Green, nobodies? They sustained it giving more than any of the paid people. Instead, *Freedom* have preferred to boost people like Karl Walter, the fascist granddad of Nicolas, passing him off as an anarchist.

Those rescued in the book from oblivion and in some cases calumny by the approved writers of Freedom Press history, are nobody and nothing, however many years they supported it and in some cases founded. What a contempt for the readership from people who, pressed, admit they do not believe in Anarchism.

So, lies, malice, falsehood, calumny, instability and inconsistency give a "convincing impression of a certain type of anarchist personality", do they? If they think that, why do they produce an allegedly anarchist paper? The answer: they ponce off the ideology for direct financial or indirect careerist motives.

Black Flag no. 208 [mid 1996]

4. Albert Meltzer and the fight for working class history

Albert Meltzer was a central figure in the development of the Kate Sharpley Library, both practically (laying out and distributing the bulletin and pamphlets) and also philosophically. His concern at seeing the history of anarchism rewritten to suit other people's agendas was part of the motivation for the founding of the Library.[1] It also connected with the rest of his anarchism: class-conscious, committed to liberation from below, sceptical of 'experts' and unafraid of criticising them.

His historical writing, like all of his writing, was punchy, humorous and anecdotal. 'Our historical judgement was criticised as based only on anecdotal history from veterans but knowing how conventional history is concocted I doubt if it suffered from that.'[2] Albert wrote anarchist history from his own experience and the accounts of comrades he knew. He did not have the leisure (or the patience) to comb through archives. He also knew that relying on published sources could write the people who made up the anarchist movement out of history. To Albert, most academics had proven themselves incapable of understanding the anarchist movement: 'Working-class theoreticians who express and formulate theories are totally ignored as of no consequence: what they say is attributed to the next available "Intellectual".'[3] Albert was sceptical of both academic methodology: '"Research" often means looking up dated reference books, and passing it off as knowledge.'[4] and also their motivation: 'Anarchism has become fair game for those eager to climb on the academic gravy train'.[5]

History, and the writing of history, was deeply political to Albert. 'Many would like to filch the history of the Anarchist movement.'[6] A shining example of this – and the 'sectarian' riposte – came in *Black Flag*'s response to Keith Paton's 'Alternative Liberalism : in search of ideological neighbours' suggesting Young Liberals adopt 'non-violent' anarchism. Paton wrote "'I'm not talking about the violent or destructive currents of anarchism or the anarchism that tail-ends Marxism and is obsessed with preventing the 'emasculation' (sic) of the revolution... We claim a long and largely honourable tradition: e.g. it was we anarchists whom the Bolsheviks first attacked in post-revolutionary Russia, April 1918; e.g. the social creativity of the anarchist influenced workers and peasants in Spain in 1936-37, before snuffed out by the troops of right and left; May 68 to some extent[...]" *Black Flag* responded 'Humbug! "We anarchists" whom the Bolsheviks attacked, "we anarchists" who fought in Spain, and struggled ever since – what have "we" to do with you? Or are you pretending that it was "Peace News" types that fought in Russia and Spain? What with, bunches of posies?'[7]

Albert pointed out the positive value of history – and its contested nature – in his review of *British Syndicalism* by Bob Holton: 'The histories of whole peoples were wiped out for precisely the same reason that the history of the working class movement in recent times is wiped out: it does not suit the conquerors for it to be known, because traditions keep alive the spirit of revolt.'[8]

The study of anarchism has ballooned since Albert's death. Much solid history has been written and, importantly, published (not all of it by academics). Those of us who work on the history of the anarchist movement – a history from below if ever there was one – will keep digging. If we move on from Albert's anecdotal approach to history, we would do well not to forget his scepticism. It would be unfortunate to leave history (or theory) to the 'experts' only to find ourselves lamenting, like the 'uncontrollable' from the Iron Column, 'maybe we have failed to make ourselves understood'.[9]

Notes

1, See 'The Kate Sharpley Library Then, Now and Next: An Interview with Barry Pateman' *KSL: Bulletin of the Kate Sharpley Library* No. 63-64, October 2010 http://www.katesharpleylibrary.net/0vt50w.

2, Describing *Cuddon's Cosmopolitan Review*, in chapter 12, pages 182–3 of *I couldn't paint golden angels* (1996) http://www.katesharpleylibrary.net/ngf32q.

3, Albert Meltzer 'Only a few intellectuals' *Black Flag* vol.3, no.19 page 7 (April 1975)

4, Albert Meltzer *I couldn't paint golden angels* chapter 9, page 166 http://www.katesharpleylibrary.net/6djj4k.

5, Albert Meltzer *Anarchism: arguments for and against*, 2nd edition (2000), page 18.

6, Albert Meltzer 'What is the anarchist movement?' *Black Flag* vol.7, no.7 page 36 (Autumn 1984).

7, Anonymous but probably Albert Meltzer 'Roon 'n' aboot: Keith Paton knew my father' *Black Flag* vol.4, no.13 page 4 (1977).

8, *Cienfuegos Press Anarchist Review* no.2 page 16 (1977).

9, An uncontrollable from the Iron Column, 'The Iron Column, militarisation and the revolutionary future of Spain' [AKA *A day mournful and overcast*] in Abel Paz *The story of the Iron Column* (2011) page 188.

KSL Bulletin **76 (October 2013)**

5. When Albert died (personal recollections)

It's twenty years since Albert Meltzer died. Since I was there, I'd like to share what I remember. I went to the Solidarity Federation conference in Weston-super-Mare in 1996. I had a book of Nestor Makhno's essays and a return ticket. I was there on the final morning, I think all the conference stuff had been done, and people were gathering in the lounge. Albert suffered his stroke. I went with him in the ambulance. It seemed the obvious thing to do, since I'd known him for several years.

The hospital was on the edge of town, low rise with small trees round it. I well remember the ward and its waiting room. I went in everyday, I can't remember for how many days. I remember eating in the canteen, so I assume there were morning and afternoon visiting hours. Albert never regained consciousness, but he'd move in his sleep.

I also remember the hill over the road, which was a bit of a refuge for me. There were cowslips in the grass, a church and the stump of a windmill. The ridge of rock carried on to make an island out in the channel. I can hardly remember anything more about what else I did, though I did meet up with a local comrade.

I looked at that book of Makhno essays recently. The bookmark was a single ticket back to Weston-super-Mare. I must've gone away to give in my notice and move my stuff. The next day I got a phone call at breakfast time from Stuart to say that Albert had died. That was the 7th of May. After that, I stayed in Albert's flat in Lewisham and did whatever I could to help Stuart and Simon. They had their hands full, given that they had the funeral to organise – horse-drawn hearse, jazz band and all. And that was just the procession.

We gave Albert exactly the send-off he wanted. A full house, and no worthy cliches. The thing I remember best is the comedian. Noel James did a comedy routine at the crematorium. I don't know if this was planned, and he had nerves of steel, of if this was a beautiful ad lib. He turned his soft guitar case into an elephant's head (the neck of the guitar making the elephant's trunk) and launched into a long and very involved anecdote, taking it to the point where no-one knew what he was going on about. So he stopped. "If I'm going to die on stage, I'm in the right place, aren't I?" That brought the house down.

Less amusing was the carping in print (or was it sniping?) from some of those associated with Freedom Press at that time. We probably shouldn't have been surprised, given the long-standing disagreements involved. It was distasteful and it felt to me that there was arrogance as well as bad timing involved. It was insinuated that Albert's support for the Spanish resistance, or Stuart Christie in particular, was imaginary. *The Albert Memorial: The Anarchist Life and Times of Albert Meltzer* by Phil Ruff with contributions from other comrades (first edition from 1997) corrects some of these 'misunderstandings'.

Sometimes I regret that Albert isn't around to laugh at some of the epic missing-the-point that you see in academic writing about anarchism. I'm sure he'd have been amused to hear a contemporary professor tell him that as he's not a philosopher, he's not *qualified* to contribute to anarchist thinking! Of course, his comrades – and those he has inspired – would beg to differ.

Though we miss him, we shouldn't be sad. He lived – and enjoyed – a life devoted to a cause. The tributes paid to him after his death give some indication of his contribution. And what did he leave undone? His autobiography tells us (as with the sign-painter in Heinrich Heine's short story): he never did paint any golden angels. But who would have it any other way?

John Patten

Note

A video of the funeral procession, service and wake is on Stuart Christie's facebook page: https://www.facebook.com/photo.php?v=512868175425287.

Originally illustrated by a photo of red and black flags at Albert Meltzer's funeral by Col Longmore http://www.katesharpleylibrary.net/q83cvd. See back cover.

KSL Bulletin **86–87 (May 2016)**